GORDON WALLACE

My Ranger Years

SEQUOIA NATIONAL PARK 1935–1947

Co-published by Sequoia Natural History Association
and Lamplighter Press

© 1993, Gordon Wallace, Prescott, Arizona

Written by Gordon Wallace
Project coordinated by John Palmer
Edited by Susan McDonald Tasaki
Designed by Carole Thickstun
Typesetting by Andresen Graphic Services, Tucson

Library of Congress Cataloging-in-Publication Data

Wallace, Gordon, 1909–
  My ranger years / Gordon Wallace.
    p.   cm.
    ISBN 1-878441-04-3 (pbk. : alk. paper)
    1. Wallace, Gordon, 1909–   . 2. Park rangers—California—Sequoia
National Park—Biography.   3. United States. National Park Service—
Officials and employees—Biography.   4. Sequoia National Park (Calif.)—
History. I. Title.
  SB481.6.W34A3
  333.78'3'092—dc20
  [B]   92-25166
                                                  CIP

ISBN 1-878441-0403

dedicated to the memory of
COLONEL JOHN R. WHITE
longtime guardian *extraordinaire*
of
Sequoia National Park

Tower Rock from the Ranger Pasture at Lewis Camp

My heart is where the hills fling up,

Green garlands to the day.

'Tis where the blue lake brims her cup,

The sparkling rivers play.

Wendell Phillips Stafford

RANGER WALLACE AT HOME IN THE KERN CANYON

Contents

Foreword

For wilderness travellers, particularly those who favor the Sequoia-Kings region, Ranger Wallace's fascinating and authentic book is required reading. I know of no other account of a ranger's experiences and adventures that so clearly depicts the unique activities of a national park service ranger in the High Sierra.

I found utterly fascinating his vivid descriptions of exciting near-disastrous wilderness accidents, amusing incidents, the changing of seasons, and his mountain romances. Together with the keen portrayal of his life at park headquarters and under the Big Trees of The Giant Forest, Wallace's book presents a readable and realistic account of the all-round responsibilities unique to a mountain ranger in the 1930s and 40s.

His imaginative writing about the scenic features, the trails, the campsites, and the backcountry travellers has reminded me poignantly of my own High Sierra activities that were taking place during this same period. It also made me recall with nostalgia the dozen or more park rangers, packers, trail crews, and the colorful John R. White, park superintendent, all of whom were well known to me. Wallace has interwoven all this and more into a tale of his many adventures during the six seasons he patrolled the superb high country of Sequoia National Park and his other experiences during the years he served on the park's protective force.

It was fifty years ago that I first met Gordon Wallace at his ranger station near Lewis Camp in the spectacularly beautiful Kern River Canyon. It is the most picturesque of all backcountry NPS stations I know, and he fitted in well— immediately impressing me as a sterling example of what I thought a ranger should be. Bound by our mutual interests, he and I have kept in touch during the intervening years, and thus it is that I have the pleasure to heartily recommend this fine, readable, true-to-life narrative.

NORMAN B. LIVERMORE, JR.
Calistoga, Calif. June 1992

N.B. (Ike) Livermore is well known for his more than sixty years close association with the High Sierra as a packer and owner of pack trains on both sides of the southern Sierra Nevada, and for his part in influencing key High Sierra wilderness decisions during the years (1967–1974) when he was California's Secretary for Resources under Governor Reagan.

THE KAWEAHS FROM LITTLE FIVE LAKES

MORAINE LAKE

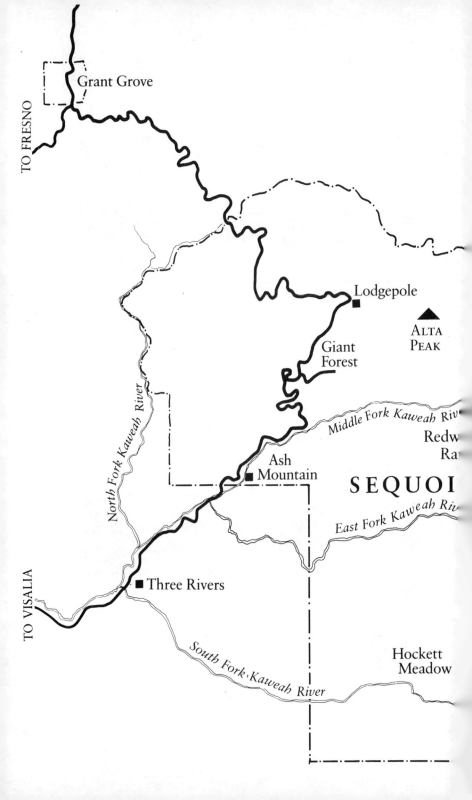

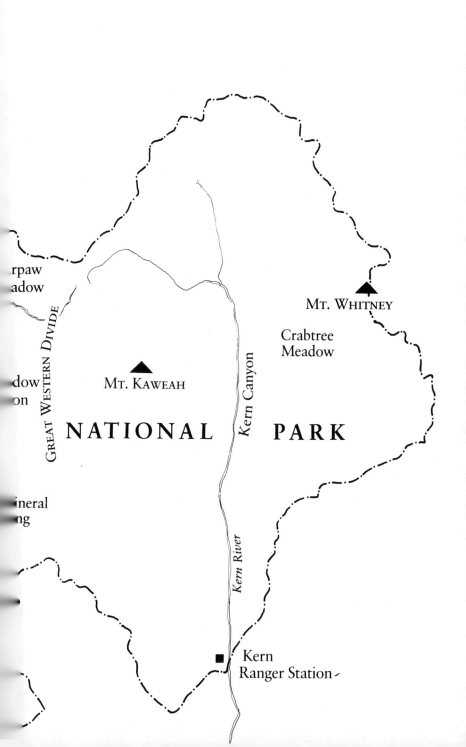

1

The CCC Connection

My first glimpse of the Giant Sequoias, in 1934, was overwhelming. The incredible size, perfect symmetry, and rich beauty of their cinnamon-colored bark and blue-green foliage filled me with an awe that long familiarity with them has not diminished. The Giant Forest Plateau—with its legions of mature Sequoias and hosts of magnificent representatives of other species of trees spread over some eighteen hundred acres—seemed indeed a heaven on earth.

To reach the Giant Forest, I had traversed a sinuous route from Salt Creek, a nineteen-mile-long drive that rose more than a vertical mile through several life zones before topping out at 6,400 feet in Giant Forest Village. It was spectacular, unlike anything I'd ever seen before.

My ramble through the woods alone in the moonlight that first night was truly an experience that remains vivid in my memory to this day. The trail I took began at the village and followed a fairly level gradient through the forest to Moro Rock, two miles distant. The silent forest was silvered by moonlight, and the only life that stirred was an occasional deer, who would momentarily lift its head from its browsing, twitch its ears, and gaze inquisitively and unafraid at me as I walked slowly along the trail. I felt myself to be a trespasser in their realm, yet blessed to have somehow merged in spirit with those wonderful specimens of the animal and plant kingdoms.

Several weeks later I made another visit to the Giant Forest Plateau. It was about mid-September when two of my tentmates and I caught a ride one weekend to the Marble Fork CCC Camp, well up into the forest. We began our eight-mile hike there, following a trail along the Marble Fork of the Kaweah that wound up eventually at Wolverton Meadow. There we picked up the precipitous trail to Heather and Emerald lakes, reaching the latter about sunset. We had each finagled a few sandwiches from the kitchen at Salt Creek Camp, our fare for twenty-four hours. We carried no canteens as streams and lakes provided clear, cool, and refreshing water. That evening, we built a small campfire on the shore of Emerald Lake and talked a bit; then, blanketless, we curled up around the fire on the ground in the clothes we wore and slept the best we could.

In the morning, we ate the last of our sandwiches and, tenderfeet that we were in these mountains, had the temerity to tackle the chimney on the north side of Alta Peak. Clawing our way up this steep, narrow declivity and dodging rocks dislodged by the uppermost climber, we somehow made it safely and breathlessly to the top. We had conquered our first mountain peak—over 11,000 feet high. It was well worth the exposure and effort, as Alta Peak stands alone and well apart from its sisters in the nearby Great Western Divide; hence, its summit affords a magnificent 360-degree view of the entire Middle Fork and Marble Fork watersheds.

From there, it was, as they say, downhill all the way for twelve miles, and we coasted in high spirits into Giant Forest and caught a ride to Salt Creek Camp, completing our first High Sierra adventure.

The story of how I came to this mountain wonderland that changed my life began on a balmy southern California day in June 1934, when destiny decreed that I be seated on the left side of a certain streetcar. This may seem unlikely, but it was that simple—and fateful. As we rolled along Los Angeles Street en route to the Pacific Electric Terminal in Los Angeles, I noticed a large crowd, more than a hundred men, milling around in front of a building near the streetcar tracks. The most likely explanation was that some kind of job was available, so I got off at the next corner and went back to investigate.

Times were hard; the Great Depression was at its lowest ebb, and I was among the millions who were out of work. My last job pruning grapefruit trees around Indio had petered out early in the month, and I was practically broke. I decided to spend some of my remaining cash to ride over to Pasadena on the big red interurban cars and hit up my most-recent employer for the wages due me. (He had been unable at the time he laid us all off to pay our last week's wages and had promised to do so later.) For once during those trying days, fortune smiled a little; he had just enough cash on hand to square his debt to me—a matter of some twenty dollars. With that I planned to follow through in a day or two on a decision I had made to bum my way back to Kansas where I was born and raised and had a number of close and caring relatives. I just wasn't making it in California and was ready to hop a freight east to give my native state a try, twenty-four years after my original appearance there.

When I reached the fringe of the crowd, I asked one of the men what was going on, and he told me that applications were being taken inside for enrollment in the Civilian Conservation Corps. This program, part of President Franklin Delano Roosevelt's New Deal, had first come to my attention at its inception in the spring of 1933. Although mildly interested, I was occupied at the time attending junior college and thereafter with long hours of work as an auto-park attendant; the CCC was a last resort. Now, I was in dire straits, and here

3

was that last resort, practically flung at me by Fate. I joined the crowd and waited my turn for an interview.

I had been standing there barely five minutes when someone from inside appeared in the doorway and asked those who could type to come forward. I did so, and was escorted at once into the inner sanctum, where I was enrolled in the CCC without delay. My qualification was genuine: I had taken a year of typing in high school (probably the most useful thing I learned in my four years) and had subsequently increased my dexterity by doing a lot of writing at the typewriter.

My skills were employed to process new enrollees at the staging center at Fort MacArthur in San Pedro. Tours of duty were to begin early in July, and I was instructed to appear at Fort MacArthur, ready for work, on July second. This left me a week or so to straighten out my affairs (what affairs?), collect my thoughts (I had nothing else), take my ease at the beach in Santa Monica, and enjoy a life free from worry, for a change.

I arrived at Fort MacArthur, wearing my only suit and pair of shoes and carrying a small handbag with a few personal things. I was outfitted right away with a complete set of clothing and toilet articles, and, as a member of the processing cadre, was assigned to a private barracks room. However, typical of bureaucratic wisdom, my typing skills were never used. Instead, I measured incoming enrollees' heights and weights and filled out forms for several weeks. When the rush subsided, I was assigned to other duties of a housekeeping nature, the most significant and responsible of which was the cleanup of the old coast artillery batteries that overlooked the sea.

I worked with Major Blair, camp commandant, in processing the new enrollees, and after that, closely with Captain Gearhart, a young, personable, energetic West Point graduate. After several days of a number of random post assignments, Captain Gearhart put me in charge of a detail of about thirty men, to clean up one of the emplacements. As the leader of a crew that consisted entirely of World War I veterans old enough to be my father, I had some concern about the way we would work together. I explained to the men what we had to do and how I wanted them to do it. I supervised them closely and treated them with consideration and without condescension. As a result, they did a whale of a job, responding well to the demands of the project. When Captain Gearhart, himself a stickler for excellence, saw the job we had done, he kept us on that assignment until all the batteries had been policed. That completed, the captain assigned me to other leadership roles for the remainder of my six-weeks tour at Fort Mac-Arthur.*

My days at Fort MacArthur were among the most pleasant of my life. It was an ideal interlude: the work was both interesting and challenging, and there was plenty of time for recreation. My quarters were comfortable and private, and the food, served cafeteria-style, was varied, tasty, and plentiful. I quickly made new friends among the CCC cadre and enjoyed their camaraderie, dates and parties with the girls of San Pedro, and many an afternoon at nearby Cabrillo Beach.

The staging operation at Fort MacArthur ended in mid-August. We had processed several thousand CCC enrollees and sent them on to camps throughout the state; now it was our turn to go. Those of us who were judged to have handled our jobs well were given a choice of California camps. I considered two: Yosemite and Sequoia. I had never seen either, but had read and heard great things about both. Three of my camp friends and I talked things over and decided to go to Sequoia as a group, along with the other enrollees being sent there to form a new camp. It was a happy choice.

We were assigned to Salt Creek CCC Camp, newly established in the rugged valley of the Middle Fork of the Kaweah River, about three miles below the entrance to Sequoia National Park. The CCC was to be employed to construct a truck trail up Salt Creek to Cinnamon Gap on the western

---

*Many years later, I read that Captain Gearhart had become a three-star general serving as chief of the Pentagon's Congressional Liaison Office on Capitol Hill. I was not surprised at his success.

flank of Case Mountain. This trail would provide fire-fighting access to an area that had heretofore been without protection from grass, brush, or forest fires—a genuine conservation project. The camp was located on a little plateau just above the confluence of Salt Creek with the Middle Fork. In the foothills of the Sierra Nevada, at an elevation of only 1,000 feet, the intense summer heat turned most of the vegetation brown and dried out the earth. It was not the cool, green, high forest we had hoped for, but was an exciting opportunity nonetheless.

After a few days of settling in, we were lined up one morning by the camp superintendent, who was in charge of the project, and told to pick up a tool from the stacks of picks, shovels, mattocks, and axes laid out in front of us. I was standing there with my buddies, Ted, Al, and Joe. As we eyed one another, a common thought seemed to take shape: *This isn't for us. We're used to taking charge. Let's hold off and see what happens.* The tools eventually ran out and left us standing there empty-handed. When the superintendent saw us, he said, "Each of you fellows take a group of men and report with them to a foreman, and he'll tell you what to do." Whereupon he divided the men into groups, and away we went. And that is how Ted and Al and Joe and I became leaders at the Salt Creek Camp.

The foremen were older, local men, also employed in conservation under a different aegis, the Emergency Conservation Works (ECW). The CCC enrollees, directly supervised by CCC leaders and assistant leaders, worked at their direction. Within a few weeks, Ted, Al, Joe, and I were all officially promoted from enrollee status at thirty dollars a month to assistant leaderships at thirty-six dollars per month. Several months later, Ted, Al, and I were officially made leaders, at the top CCC pay of forty-five dollars a month. This was all clear, since shelter, clothing, food, transportation, and medical attention were furnished. Joe's status did not change: he remained an assistant leader.

The work was novel and stimulating; I welcomed the responsibility and the challenge of taking a crew of twenty-five

CCC Workers Building the Salt Creek Truck Trail

CCC Leader Wallace and Crew

to thirty men and converting a pristine hillside studded with mountain oak, buckeye, brush, boulders, and granite outcroppings into a good, smooth, well-graded road capable of carrying truck traffic and fire-fighting equipment. To assist in the heaviest of this work when I needed it, I had a caterpillar-bulldozer and a dump truck at my disposal. At the finishing stage, I personally handled a specially constructed slope board to pass on the inslope and road width and order any adjustment before leapfrogging my crew past others to the next section in our advance.

The course of the roadbed was already surveyed and marked with cut-and-fill stakes when we came onto a new section. I would send a few men ahead to fell trees and clear brush. Then I would oversee the dynamiting of stumps and rocky outcroppings too large for removal by pick, shovel, mattock, and crowbar, tools with which most of the crew worked. Often it was necessary to install culverts to carry the water from small streams, as well as build rock walls in places where the course was too precipitous for a fill. For these special tasks, I soon learned who I could depend upon to do a good job. There were few moments to completely relax; I was kept busy instructing new workers on how to handle their tools, helping remove boulders, preparing dynamite charges and setting them off, checking on the operations of my brush-cutting crew, and overseeing the removal of dirt from cuts and its transfer to fills. Ours was a creative endeavor, and I took considerable pride in what my crew and I had accomplished as we completed each of our sections along the road.

There were about one hundred fifty of us in camp, ranging in age from eighteen to forty-three. Most of us were in our mid-twenties. We came from diverse backgrounds, but had one thing in common: a need for gainful employment. We formed a micro-society whose members existed on the same socio-economic level.

Most of us came from the Los Angeles metropolitan area. Al and Joe were typical: young, healthy, aspiring, but having a hard time making ends meet with little or no employment. Ted, whose full name was Theodore Vittorio Peshehonoff, became my close, steadfast, lifelong friend. He had a colorful background. His father had been a man of great wealth and position whose factories had furnished virtually all the boots worn by Russian soldiers in World War I, as well as other leather goods. The Russian Revolution forced eleven-year-old Ted and his father and mother to leave everything but their silver behind and flee for their lives in the late spring of 1919. With the assistance of a loyal guide they were able, after many hardships, to make the long trek by horseback across the snow-clad forests and wasteland of Siberia to Vladivostok, the haven of "White" refugees. A year or so later they immigrated to America, ultimately settling in Los Angeles. When I met Ted's father in 1936, he was the proprietor of a small neighborhood shoe-repair shop, a cobbler whose descent from a position of great wealth, culture, and prestige had not embittered him in the least. He struck me as a friendly, open, outgoing, serious man endowed with a saving sense of humor; I liked him. His son Ted was a different sort, a charming rogue: impetuous, emotional, devil-may-care, and personable. He was a highly intelligent human and an unwaveringly loyal friend who enriched my life.

There were others in camp who were also not exactly run-of-the-mill, but who represented the widespread social and economic consequences of the Great Depression. For example, Taylor presided over the infirmary. He had been the victim of a mishap on the firing range during his third year at West Point. The result was a paralysis of the nerves of his right eye and ear and a subsequent discharge from the U.S. Military Academy, because he could no longer meet the high physical standards required of its cadets.

The kitchen and mess hall, the recreation hall and orderly room, the infirmary, and the latrine were all housed in hurriedly constructed wooden buildings. The workers slept in old canvas squad tents from World War I days, with wooden platforms laid for the flooring. Each contained a centrally positioned heating stove, and five double bunks with space for individual footlockers underneath. This arrangement was reasonably comfortable; even when it got nippy in the winter and snowed a bit, we were warm enough inside with our stove and outside with warm clothing. Among my tentmates were two Blacks and three Hispanics: we got along well together. There is nothing like mutual hardship and deprivation to make men brothers under the skin.

Although our pay was minuscule, carefully budgeted, it was enough to let us enjoy some good times. After supper during hot weather, we drifted down to the Mountain Oak Inn, about a quarter-mile from camp. There we sat and talked and sipped lemonade to our heart's content until it was time to go to bed. It was a delightful respite from the hot day's labor.

There was also a good swimming hole in the nearby river, which I frequented. On the near side of the river, just above the hole, rose a bluff that issued a challenge to me every time I came near; and each time I would be drawn inexorably to meet that challenge by hurling myself off the bluff into the water twenty-eight feet below. I was by no means an accomplished high diver, so this must have been little more than a manifestation of youthful daredeviltry. (Fortunately I was smart enough to explore these watery depths for hidden hazards before engaging in this adventure.)

Every Saturday and Sunday, a large stake-body truck fitted with wooden benches took us the thirty miles or so into Visalia for afternoons and evenings of recreation. This usually consisted of movies and café-hopping. There was a bit of drinking, and sometimes we were carried away with youthful exuberance.

For some of us the principal pastime in camp was poker. We had some great games, even though the stakes were necessarily small. Bull sessions about everything under the sun were ongoing. Sometimes six or seven of us held forth in the back room of the infirmary for many hours before dispersing early in the morning. Best of all was the camaraderie that permeated our lives together. It was good to be alive and young and healthy and to enjoy one another's company.

The months passed. A crisp and colorful autumn turned to winter, which in turn gave way to spring. Ah, yes, spring in the foothills of the Sierra Nevada—in my view no more beauty can be found anywhere in the world than in that time and place. The blossoming redbud, buckeye, ceanothus, and yucca, together with a great profusion of variegated wild-flowers dominated by lupine, spread over the terrain like a beautiful carpet. It is a sight that, once seen, will hold you captive forever.

As time went on, however—even though contented at Salt Creek Camp—I felt a need to move on to something bigger and better. I was hooked on this environment and wanted to remain in it; when it came to my attention that there were temporary ranger jobs to be filled up in the park beginning May first, I decided to apply for one, in spite of the fact that in all my life I had spent only four months in the mountains. In fact, I had never even been in a national park until ECW Foreman Hart took me up to Giant Forest. What I saw and felt then and on the Alta Peak hike changed my mind about life in the mountains, though. It now appeared to me that I could do a lot worse than spend a summer in Sequoia.

So, about the first of April, after supper one evening, I walked up the highway to Ash Mountain, the headquarters of Sequoia National Park, and knocked on the door of the residence of the park superintendent. He answered my knock and showed considerable surprise at seeing this roughly clad CCC boy standing at his doorstep. Quickly recovering, he asked, "What can I do for you, young man?"

I replied, "I want a job in your park this summer; and I hear that there may be some temporary ranger openings."

"Oh, you do, do you? Well, come on inside and we'll talk about it," he responded.

That is how I met Colonel John R. White, the flamboyant, somewhat eccentric, vigorous, extremely capable man who ran his show the way he wanted, come hell or high water. He took an immediate liking to me and I to him, and our relationship was solid and warm until the day he died many years later. His parting words, "You come up to headquarters in a day or two and see Captain Ford Spigelmyre, the chief ranger. I'll speak to him about you," encouraged me greatly.

I wasted no time in making contact with Chief Ranger Spigelmyre. As a consequence of my interview with him, I came away with a promise of a temporary ranger position for the summer season, to begin on May first. It was all so smoothly and easily done that I had to suspect the fine hand of the park superintendent in the matter.

Thus it was that on April 29 I made a trip to Merced to buy the uniform required by my new status. I had been told that the B. B. McGinnis Company in that city was the place to go to get outfitted. By the time I got there, however, the store was closed for the day, so I looked around for a place to spend the night. I made my way to the Merced version of skid-row on Highway 99, where I located a somewhat dilapidated hotel that offered me a room for a dollar, which I took at once, as it was all I could afford.

The following morning I was on hand when the store opened, eager to get togged out in proper uniform tie, shirt, riding breeches, hat, and boots. The official shirt was cotton, long-sleeved, and light grey in color; the riding breeches were forest green; and the hat a dark-grey, hard-brimmed Stetson. The dress boots, however, were the star of this ensemble: beautifully crafted in soft cordovan leather reaching to just below the knee, they took a brilliant shine. This uniform had real class, and it gave the park ranger of that day an image that made him the object of admiration among females and respect and envy among men. I walked out of B. B. McGinnis without paying for this uniform. I must have seemed a good risk to be allowed to pay for it out of my future salary of one hundred forty dollars per month.

I returned to the Salt Creek CCC Camp and spent the last night of my CCC career there. The ten months I spent in the CCC provided me with one of the most rewarding experiences of my life; it gave me hope in a time of need and pointed me in a direction that enriched me immeasurably.

2

The Giant Forest

Resplendent in my new uniform, I reported to Chief Ranger Spigelmyre early next morning, May 1, 1935, to begin my duties as a temporary ranger in Sequoia National Park. The Civilian Conservation Corps was the bridge between that day on the streetcar not quite a year ago and this. I knew very little about what I might be in for, but the prospect appeared inviting and challenging, and I was eager to get on with it.

I signed a few papers and was quickly issued a badge, collar ornaments, and cooking equipment. Then I was introduced to Ranger Sam Clark. Before I knew it, Sam and I were in a government pickup headed for Giant Forest, which was to be my duty station.

Sam Clark was a good man and a fine ranger. In his midthirties, somewhat taller than average, slender and vigorous in movement, he looked the part. Intelligent, personable, and outgoing, he was a natural for meeting the public. He broke me in during my first few weeks on the job. Methodically and painstakingly he drove me over all the roads on the Giant

Forest Plateau and explained my responsibilities. He provided the booklets and brochures and volumes of special information whose contents I must be familiar with to properly serve the visiting public at my post at the information station.

That first day he taught me the importance of making frequent contact with the chief ranger's office, not only to make sure that the telephone and lines were functioning, but to be available for any emergency that may have arisen while away from station. Because radio was not yet employed, on our way to Giant Forest that first morning, we stopped at Hospital Rock, Big Fern, Amphitheater Point, and Deer Ridge to test the telephone system. Late that afternoon, Sam also escorted me to Round Meadow and instructed me in the recording and reporting of weather data.

In the meantime, I was introduced to the Last Hill Dormitory, which was to be my home for the next five months. On the Generals Highway about a hundred yards below the Giant Forest Information Station, the post office, and the Village Coffee Shop, it had been built a few years previously as a dormitory for snow-removal crews. A substantial building that housed the heavy equipment required stood next door. There was running water and even a shower in the dormitory, but no inside toilet; the privy was perched precariously on the slope behind and below the level of the dormitory. Scrambling back up required care and strenuous effort.

After a cookstove was installed in the dormitory, I began to prepare my own meals. At the beginning of the season as many as five of us bedded down in the one large living room; two of the others eventually went afield to their summer assignments, and three of us remained. Aside from its convenient location, the Last Hill Dormitory was by far the best bachelor quarters in the park, a thoroughly satisfactory, even desirable summer residence. More importantly, it became the scene of great camaraderie and the fostering of lifelong friendships.

Sam Clark and his wife Hazel occupied the district ranger's residence; the other permanent ranger on the Giant Forest Plateau, John G. Sinclair, a transplant from Yosemite, lived in the ranger residence at the entrance to Lodgepole Campgrounds. The two of them ran the show in Giant Forest and Lodgepole during the off-season, each often working both areas. Jack Sinclair became my supervisor shortly after I arrived on the job.

Jack was a park ranger who loved his work as few rangers do, and that is saying a lot. When I first met him, he was almost forty years old, a big strong man with a sort of lumbering gait that belied his speed of foot on a mountain trail. A hardy Scot, he was equally fond of tea and his pipe, which seemed to be in his hand more often than it was in his mouth. Jack had a habit of holding a slightly clenched fist, first finger pressed against his lips, and staring vacantly into space as if in deep thought. This gave a lot of people the impression that he was absent-minded; he was in fact quite agile mentally, as well as a very conscientious worker. He went about the task of overseeing my education as a knowledgeable ranger with singular dedication. Day after day as we worked together, he plied me with questions about the park and its resources, which kept me studying the literature, not only in spare moments while on duty at the Information Station in Giant Forest, but during my off-duty hours as well. Through Sam's and Jack's efforts and guidance, I became well prepared to answer the questions of inquisitive tourists throughout the summer season.

I had been on the job only a week when a tourist appeared whose visit made such an impression that it stayed in my memory all these years. In charge of the Giant Forest Information Station that day, I was busying myself outside when a large, new, custom-built convertible sedan topped the hill. Driven by a liveried chauffeur, it was a Pierce-Arrow that had been constructed so that the canopy over its rear section could be opened, leaving the tonneau completely open to the sky above. There, standing upright and grasping the lap-robe rail in front of them, were a sixtyish man and his wife, rubbernecking at the Big Trees with an abandon that would shame a hayseed cast for the first time into the canyons of Manhattan. As they approached in their car, their eyes turned heavenward and their heads swiveling from side to side, the gentleman exclaimed over and over, "My, my! This is wonderful! Perfectly marvelous! Incredible!"

When the car stopped at the station and they sat down, I went over to see if I could be of assistance. That's when I noticed that he wore an expensive imported-tweed golf suit and no shoes! During a pleasant conversation I learned that this dignified, amiable old German was the president of a large bank in Milwaukee. He was out West seeing the sights in comfort, and he was really seeing them. We talked for perhaps twenty minutes, during which he asserted that he envied me my life and wished he could trade jobs with me. The Sequoias had overwhelmed him and given him a spiritual uplift as nothing in nature had ever done before. The last I saw of them, he and his wife were standing upright again in the tonneau, hatless and shoeless, wagging their heads from side to side, straining to see the tops of the Sequoias as the Pierce-Arrow disappeared around a curve in the road. This man and his wife were but the forerunners of countless others over the years who revealed similar thoughts and emotions as they fell, with reverence and awe, under the spell of the giant Sequoias.

What, really, is the essence of the *Sequoiadendron giganteum* that inspires man with an experience that can be felt so deeply in his soul, yet can be only inadequately verbalized? Can it be their size? Their overwhelming measurements certainly put puny man in his place, but statistics lack life. Can it be their ethereal beauty? To many there is nothing in the forest that remotely compares with the magnetism of these great, symmetrical trees. That certainly has to be part of it.

Then there is their age, as they are not only the largest, but with a rare exception, the very oldest of living things. Together with the Bristlecone pine, *Pinus longaeva*, they are the last vestige of an age long past, a venerable relic in the present age, a bridging between two evolutionary eras. The

Big Trees are perhaps as close as we come on earth to a living relationship with eternity.

Their cultural aspect, especially to Americans living on a newly developed continent too young to have the traditional antiquities of older cultures, is also a factor. Here we have in nature monuments to match, if not surpass, the greatest efforts of man as presented by the gothic cathedrals and the ruins of ancient Greece and Rome. The discovery of the Big Trees destroys forever the idea that culture derives only from the works of man.

I had a diverse group of duties on the job. For example, the month of May is normally the slowest time of the year on the Giant Forest Plateau because it is between seasons. The snow cover gradually disappears at this time, exposing the deterioration and debris that results from severe winter temperatures and the activities of human beings. Because maintenance personnel did not take up summer stations until later in the season, the ranger filled in.

So it was that day after day I shoveled snow to afford access to buildings, swept sidewalks, gathered trash, raked gutters, cleaned toilets and policed rest rooms, painted and replaced signs, repaired equipment, cleaned out park cabins, washed windows, maintained Coleman lanterns and fire extinguishers, stored winter paraphernalia, distributed outdoor wastebaskets, cleaned up campgrounds, set up trail register boxes, and patrolled park roads by automobile. In between I would change from my working clothes to the spotless and sartorial perfection of a ranger's uniform to meet the public at the information station that I manned most of the time. The workday knew no limits, but it always began by raising the flag at the information station about seven-thirty in the morning and taking it down at five in the evening, as well as recording and reporting weather data.

To be sure, there were chores not in the daily run-of-the-mill: a dead deer on the highway to dispose of, a lightning-set fire to corral and extinguish, and fish to restock. One day, early in the season, I found a fawn with legs still so wobbly that it had collapsed in the middle of the highway and was lying there inert when I came along. I picked it up and carried it a few steps into the woods where I set it down. When I returned an hour later to check on it, it had disappeared. And then there was the tragedy that occurred on May twenty-eighth.

My diary tells me that I was posting signs in the Hazelwood picnic area that morning when I observed several army bombers overhead. I was unaware that a few minutes later one mysteriously went into a spin and crashed on Manzanita Hill. A report quickly reached park headquarters, and the chief ranger immediately dispatched Jack Sinclair and me to the scene of the crash to take charge. We left Giant Forest Village at ten-twenty A.M., drove five miles to Lodgepole Campground, then raced afoot up the precipitous trail to the lower end of Calhoun Meadow, arriving there breathless and spent about three-quarters of an hour later.

There we found the twisted and burning wreckage of the plane, flames still licking at the bodies of the four occupants. ECW Foreman Rosenberg and his crew of six or seven CCC enrollees had been working the trail nearby and arrived ahead of us, but there was nothing to be done for the victims. We went to work extinguishing the fire and keeping the crowd at a safe distance. (Mountains and rivers and forests are no obstacles to the insatiably curious.)

When army authorities arrived, Jack and I helped with the removal and identification of the remains. Upon completion of the on-the-spot investigation by the army, the wreckage was turned over to the National Park Service to dispose of as it saw fit. At the time it seemed it might be quite a problem to remove this unsightly mess from the area and restore it to its former condition. However, we didn't take into account campers and other park visitors. They descended on the scene like a flock of buzzards and stripped the aircraft's carcass until only bones remained. Going through the campgrounds that summer to record camp census as I frequently did, I noticed that souvenirs were making their appearance at an astounding speed. A tin-snipped star from the wing, a green landing light, a piece of silk parachute, heat-twisted and flame-blackened instruments, a crumpled propeller—the list of ghoulish mementos went on and on.

By the first of June most of the snow had disappeared and things were pretty well spruced-up for the onslaught of summer visitors. They accelerated in number during the month and reached a peak on the Fourth of July weekend, a peak that was maintained through July and August and ended with the Labor Day weekend. In June other temporary rangers were assigned to help handle the crowds, and each of us soon fell heir to regular, well-defined duties: the information station, daily camp census, and motorcycle patrol of the Generals Highway between Ash Mountain Headquarters and Lost Grove on the northwestern boundary of the park.

In my opinion I had the best job of all, thanks to my previous experience as a horseman: horseback patrols over the trails that cobwebbed the Giant Forest Plateau. This routine was occasionally broken when I was charged with relieving other temporary rangers so they could take a day off. I myself took only two days off in the five months I was on the job; I just didn't want one. Along with others, I took my turn at maintaining law and order at the dances that were held six nights a week, searching for lost persons, and fighting fires. We were called on to protect the park and its visitors at any time, day or night, and I loved every minute of it. I marvelled at being paid for doing something that pleased me so much. Truly, I would not have traded places with anyone else in the world at that point in my life.

The park ranger of the time was held in high regard by the public. For the young, he embodied their dreams of romantic adventure; for the older, he personified escape from the humdrum realities of a work-a-day world. They also saw him as he actually was: friend, philosopher, and guide. At the same time, he was also policeman, fireman, woodsman, naturalist, conservator, and public educator.

There can be no doubt that the park ranger has been the

greatest single factor in the dissemination of national park policy among the American people, a policy based on three broad principles first stated in a letter of Secretary of Interior Franklin K. Lane to Stephen T. Mather, Director of the National Park Service, May 13, 1918. As modified only slightly by Secretary of the Interior Hubert Work on March 11, 1925, they endure almost intact to this day. They are: (1) that the national parks and national monuments must remain untouched by the inroads of modern civilization in order that unspoiled bits of native America may be preserved to be enjoyed by future generations as well as our own; (2) that they be set apart for the use, education, health, and pleasure of the people; and (3) that the national interest must take precedence in all decisions affecting public or private enterprise in the park.

Park rangers are the most visible link between this NPS policy and the visiting public. Theirs is the task of on-the-spot enforcement of the rules and regulations promulgated to implement policy, both as to protection of the natural environment and the preservation of law and order. Happily, the rangers of my day never had need to wear sidearms and handcuffs to discharge this responsibility, and we did not do so. In general, this speaks well for the culture of the country at that time, and in particular it reflects the tractable nature of our visiting public.*

In the beginning, I was the only occupant of the Last Hill Dormitory. Later I was joined temporarily by Ralph Wise and Jim Higgenbotham and permanently by Dave Bristow and Ned Munn. We have remained close throughout our lives. Dave was our motorcycle patrolman. About thirty, he had loafed his way through Fresno State College and then became a highly successful insurance salesman. After a few years of

---

*Contemporary rangers cope with a different society, and the gun on the hip unfortunately raises a barrier between the ranger and the visitor that dilutes the empathy that we both used to enjoy.

easy come, easy go, he decided he wanted to be a medical doctor, so he returned to Fresno State to pick up the sciences he needed for medical school. This was also his first summer as a temporary ranger. He had an impressive physique—tall and heavyset—but what was most impressive about Dave was his warm, quick smile. Highly intelligent and full of good humor, he also possessed an infinite store of common sense and the rare ability to charm all those with whom he came in contact.

Ned, a year or so younger than I, was a playboy with a different background. He became my closest pal, and we enjoyed a multitude of good times together and an intimate friendship that endured for many years. Edward (Ned) Munn had the misfortune to possess all the advantages. His father held one of the highest positions in the administration of Cook County (Chicago), Illinois. Ned had attended Dartmouth for two years and finished his last two years at the University of Chicago. He was a good friend and classmate of Raymond Ickes, the son of Harold B. Ickes, Secretary of Interior, who had given him a political appointment as a temporary ranger in Sequoia in 1934. Ned proved to be a very capable and conscientious ranger and was welcomed back for the 1935 season. A handsome and extremely personable young man, he turned down an opportunity to play professional baseball and opted to try for a stage and screen career instead. Pixyish and always ready for a good time, Ned was so full of the *joie de vivre* that he literally bounced, rather than strode, through life.

Ralph Wise was another man who came into my life at that time, and he was my surrogate father until the end of his days. He was short of stature, but long on good humor and rapier-like wit. Quick with a smile and a helping hand, he was a fine human being who, some fifteen years my senior, took a fatherly interest in me. He had spent the past four summers as a backcountry ranger stationed at the Mt. Whitney Ranger Station in the Kern District; he was reassigned to the Colony Mill Ranger Station for the 1935 season, a better arrangement for his family. Ralph was a superb horseman, and, while

21

covering the Giant Forest trails with me early in the season, taught me much that I needed still to learn about horses, trail patrol, and forest lore.

This summer also marked the beginning of my friendship with Henry G. Schmidt. Henry was a likeable fellow, rather abrupt at times in demeanor and speech, but good-hearted and intelligent. We were the same age, came out of the CCC at the same time, and held similar aspirations. By the time we had been on the job for a while, we both knew we wanted to become permanent park rangers. We used to discuss this and fantasize about someday becoming the superintendent of Sequoia National Park.*

Henry and I had been forced to mark time in our twenties as the Great Depression interfered with the pursuit of our ambitions. Both of us were continually on the lookout for the "main chance." So it was that we both took a day off, borrowed a car from Marguerite Dunaway (the girl Henry eventually married), and drove together to Fresno. There we took a civil service examination for the position of inspector with the U.S. Immigration Border Patrol, in an effort to obtain permanent employment and get a career of some kind under way.

There were others who, together with those already mentioned, combined to make the temporary ranger force of 1935 in Sequoia something special to all of us. Bernarr Bates replaced Sam Clark at the Kern Ranger Station; Jim Higgenbotham replaced Ralph Wise at Mt. Whitney Ranger Station; Kermit Guard and Andy Crosbie held forth at the Ash Mountain Checking Station; and Tom Leps and Jack Billings rounded out the group in Giant Forest.

Others helped make that summer memorable, but there was one very special person who first came to my notice when she came up to Giant Forest early in the season to become assistant to the postmaster at the village post office.

Hilda was my age. She was a comely blond of Icelandic extraction with a pleasant personality, fine figure, and more

---

*Henry actually attained that position, which he held from November 1972 to July 1975, closing out a successful NPS career.

HILDA

than her share of good looks. Although our paths crossed frequently, we both were rather reserved at first. It took a bit of time before I finally worked up enough courage to ask her for a date. In the beginning I thought of Hilda merely as a great playmate. She was warm and affectionate, a superb dancer, highly intelligent, and a fine conversationalist. Best of all we were extremely compatible. No unpleasant word ever passed between us. We rarely missed an evening together for the remainder of the summer—sipping wine, dancing, touring the deserted park roads in a borrowed topless roadster after I had chased all other vehicles off in enforcement of the eleven o'clock curfew, parking at various romantic spots, and languishing late at night before the campfire at her private tent-camp. Surrounding us was the magnificent forest through which moonbeams filtered into a fantasy world. It just doesn't get any more romantic than that.

Moreover, and important, Hilda was a good sport. She was the only female ever welcomed into the inner sanctum of our bachelor quarters at the Last Hill Dormitory. Often after the evening meal she joined Ned and Dave and me in a glass of wine or highball and lively conversation. Those were great times that invariably wound up with Hilda and I taking off for the evening dance, Ned pursuing his own romantic interest, and Dave retiring to his cot in summer hibernation.

In the light of subsequent events (which will appear in the next chapter), it is interesting to note that despite his own lack of social pursuits that summer, Dave, my good friend, God bless him, was not about to let me ease off on my own responsibilities to my steady girl. Once, after a long, uninterrupted series of nightly dates with Hilda, I decided to retire early for a change. I needed the rest. When Dave saw me creep into my sleeping bag after the evening meal, he was upset. He said, "Wally, you can't leave that girl at loose ends tonight," and he abruptly left the cabin. The next thing I knew, here came Dave down the hill on his backfiring Indian motorcycle with Hilda hanging on behind. I wouldn't go to her, so he had brought her to me. Well, what else could I do? I got dressed, we sipped some wine, and there I was on the merry-go-round again, while Dave retired to the slumber I had envisioned for myself.

About midway through the summer I came to with a start when a mutual friend, the manager of the village filling station, remarked one day, "Wally, you sure have fallen for Hilda, haven't you?" It was true, but I wasn't conscious of it until that moment, so gradual had the process been. The summer romance that I had taken rather lightly all at once took on a serious aspect from my point of view. I was completely captivated by this charming and lovely young lady, but I was never sure just how deeply she felt about me. Nevertheless, our romance glowed brightly all summer, beautifully rounding out my term in Utopia.

There was one more human component that is essential to a working man in the living of a good life: an exemplary boss. Irvin D. Kerr was that man; I never knew a finer or better-liked supervisor. Understanding, sympathetic, tactful, quiet, well-spoken, knowledgeable, and thoroughly decent, he had the respect and affection of all his subordinates. Irv was the assistant chief ranger; he and his family lived in Giant Forest Village during the summer, where he was in charge of operations in the Giant Forest District.

One incident will serve to show the kind of man he was. Ned and I were reclining one midafternoon on our cots at our home in the mountains. I'm not sure now whether our fatigue was due to some midnight escapade the night before or whether we had spent the wee hours looking for a lost tourist or chasing a recalcitrant bear through the campgrounds. No matter, there we were when Ned spotted Irv driving up in a ranger pickup. We decided we had better play possum. When Irv did not get an answer to his knock, he opened the door and looked inside. Thinking we were actually asleep, he quietly closed the door and drove off. Nothing was ever said. Whatever task he had in mind for us to perform, he found someone else to handle it.

We would do anything for this man and we cheerfully worked all hours of the day and night when the occasion demanded it. Once that summer we had the chance to do him a great favor. His young son Bobby, about four years old, wandered off into the woods late one morning and had gotten lost. When Bobby's disappearance was discovered, Irv rounded up a number of us rangers and we then searched the area. Our concern for his safety was greatly increased by the fact that bears frequented the woods behind the Kerr home, as it was near the Bear Pit that was close to where we finally found the child several hours later.*

The American black bear provided entertainment of the first magnitude for the park visitor, but he was nothing more than gall and wormwood in the cup of the ranger. The park had thoughtfully provided a grandstand to enable tourists to watch the entertaining spectacle of these brutes consuming the day's collection of garbage at a place called the Bear Pit. This pit was surrounded by a twenty-four-inch high fence of wooden rails. A good many people asked if that low, flimsy fence was effective in protecting the tourist from the bear. When they were told the fence was to protect the bear from the tourist, they were not certain just how to take it. Even so, the animals were sometimes interrupted at their noon-day feast by fool-hardy amateur photographers who insisted on closeups.

The cabin in which Dave and Ned and I lived was located along the highway that angled off from the information station on one leg of a Y, while the other leg led to the Bear Pit. Late one day, while we were preparing the evening meal, a disoriented tourist knocked at our door. Perhaps our quarters were not quite shipshape after a long and trying weekend, and perhaps we may have been slothfully relaxing in varying degrees of undress, but we were quite unprepared when, in

---

*More than a half-century after this incident, the same Bob Kerr rounded out a highly successful national park service career, retiring as a regional director, one of the service's topmost executive posts.

response to his knock, we were confronted by the innocent, but nevertheless startling, question, "Is this the Bear Pit?"

At times a bear could not get his fill at the Bear Pit, and appeased his gluttonous appetite by a nocturnal raid on the camp of some unfortunate and unsuspecting tourist. When this happened, as it all too often did, the small hours of the following night would find an unhappy ranger patrolling the camps with a lantern in one hand and a shotgun in the other.Bears can be real and even dangerous nuisances. When shotgun pellets failed to give a repeat offender cause to cease its depredations in the campgrounds, more effective action was taken. A galvanized cylindrical steel barrel mounted on two rubber-tired wheels was baited with bacon, and when the trap was sprung the bear, though unharmed, was immobilized. The ranger then hooked up the little trailer to his patrol car and took the bear for a ride that ended in release at a distance far enough away to preclude further raids by this particular culprit for the remainder of the camping season.

I had no car of my own that summer, but could not have fared better. Jack Billings, a fellow temporary ranger, owned a Chevrolet roadster that he generously placed at my disposal. It was an old model, but sturdy and dependable. There was also a Ford Model-A pickup assigned to the temporary rangers in Giant Forest for official business. Equipped with a siren, it was used to patrol the highways, ferry us to road's end to fight fires and search for lost persons, transport supplies, gather firewood, and carry out numerous other tasks. Once in a while, it served personal purposes—for example, early in the evening after a particularly hectic day when I found myself in Giant Forest already late for a spaghetti dinner to which I had been invited at Lodgepole, five miles away. Progress on the Generals Highway between those two points was slowed to a crawl by heavy traffic at the time. Anxious to reach Lodgepole without further delay, I chose to consider this an emergency; I stepped on the siren, keeping one foot on it and the other on the accelerator of the little pickup. Cars scattered like quail off to the side of the road and opened a clear path through which I sped to Lodgepole in almost record time. (Yes, perhaps irresponsible in retrospect, but lives there a young man of twenty-five with a soul so dead that he has not been seduced into such harum-scarum moments by a soaring of youthful spirit and a zest for life that knows few bounds?)

There is a machine that beckons to those with a penchant for the thrill of the wild, unimpeded, speed-created rush of air pressing strongly against the body and raising the spirits high. It, too, is part and parcel of an unrestrained *joie de vivre*. This is the motorcycle, and it was a joyful part of my life that summer.

As I have mentioned, Dave was our motorcycle patrolman. His vehicle was an old-model Indian that had given the best years of its life in the service of Sequoia National Park, and it was still going strong. I quickly learned to operate it and became Dave's relief when he took a day off. The sinuous mountain road between Ash Mountain Headquarters and Giant Forest Village is enough to frighten many drivers and their passengers from the American flatlands out of their wits, even when traversed in the relative safety of an automobile. A motorcycle is patently less safe. And the challenge I confronted as a novice motorcyclist in the patrolling of that road was exciting to say the least. I came through the experience without a scratch, but once I parted company with my vehicle in a very unceremonious manner.

There is a moderately abrupt curve along the road as it runs west just beyond the entrance to Lodgepole Camp. It appears deceptively easy to negotiate. I was breezing along on the Indian one afternoon when I came into the curve. It quickly became apparent that I just wasn't going to make it. I had no choice but to leave the road on a tangent and head across country. I bumped and careened along over a rocky and brush-strewn strip as my speed abated, but when a large pine tree I could not avoid presented its formidable bulk across my path, I decided it was time for me to take leave of my machine. I jumped off, and the Indian carried on a few feet to waver a bit and then strike the tree a glancing blow before it fell to the ground. Fortunately, neither of us suffered more damage than a scratch or two.

One day Ned asked me to help him draft a personal letter to Secretary of Interior Ickes. The subject was Lemuel A. Garrison. Lon, as he was known, had been a temporary ranger in Giant Forest the summer before, during which time Ned and he became good friends. Lon had not returned as a ranger for the summer of 1935 because he had taken an all-year position in the area as an ECW Foreman, but I had met him once when he showed up in the village.

Lon had taken the federal civil service examination and was anxious to secure a permanent NPS ranger appointment. Ned knew this and wanted to put in a good word for him with the member of the President's Cabinet who held the highest position in the federal government in the field concerned. As was mentioned earlier, he had a close connection with the Ickeses, father and son, and was not hesitant to use it. Ned also had a high regard for Lon as a ranger and as a man of integrity and ability, and the letter we composed made these points.

Before the year was out, Lon got his permanent appointment and was assigned to the Chinquapin Ranger Station in Yosemite National Park. I don't know if Lon ever learned about that letter; I never told him. I am confident though that he got his appointment because he was in line for consideration when the results of the examination placed him near the top of the eligible register. I seriously doubt that civil service rules were circumvented in this instance, but I am sure that Ned's letter did him no harm. It was a fine recommendation.*
Reluctant though I may be to refrain from further reminiscing about that idyllic summer, I have said enough to reflect what a

---

*Lon went on to carve out a highly successful career in the National Park Service, eventually holding such high positions as superintendent at Big Bend and Yellowstone national parks, director of the Midwest Region in Omaha and the Northeast Region in Philadelphia, and finally as a director of the Albright Training Academy after it was formed at the Grand Canyon National Park.

EXERCISING SQUATTER'S RIGHTS IN GIANT FOREST

FIRE FIGHTING RANGERS
(L. TO R., STANDING: WALLACE, BRISTOW, SINCLAIR;
BELOW: HIGGENBOTHAM, BILLINGS)

high-water mark it was in my life. But one marvelous adventure cannot be overlooked, for it was icing on the cake.

Colonel White, the park superintendent, was a brusque and imperious man whose military mannerisms rubbed some people the wrong way. However, he was a considerate and appreciative supervisor who went out of his way for those who served him well. He had been blessed with an exceptionally good crew of temporary rangers that summer, and to show his gratitude for our services, shortly after the Labor Day exodus of campers and tourists, he divided those of us who remained into two groups and treated us to a one-week pack trip through some of the most gorgeous country on earth.

The first group consisted of Dave Bristow, Jack Billings, and myself, with Ranger Jack Sinclair in charge. Completely outfitted with government riding and pack stock and equipment, we rode out of Wolverton Pack Station one beautiful fall morning, through the great forest of Sequoias and other magnificent conifers, and struck the High Sierra Trail. We followed this to Hamilton Lake, over Kaweah Gap to the Big Arroyo and on across the Chagoopa Plateau to what has to be one of the loveliest gems in the High Sierra, Skyparlor Meadow. Then we dipped down into the wonderland of the Kern Canyon and followed it downstream from Upper Funston Meadow to the Kern Ranger Station on Coyote Creek. Finally, we climbed over Coyote Pass and Farewell Gap and dropped down into Mineral King. The other group met us there and retraced the trail we had travelled.

It was a fabulous trip, and it ended with a ride in the back of a pickup truck that was so enchanting that even now it pierces my heart to think about it. Cushioned on sleeping bags and relaxed after a long day on horseback, with the canopy of the brilliant heavens above us, we dropped down the East Fork of the Kaweah River to Hammond and then up the highway to Ash Mountain and on to Giant Forest. It was a two-hour journey in the light of an almost-full moon that covered the land with a mantle of silver. Each turn in the road presented a kaleidoscope of unearthly beauty as we travelled down and up again through four life zones. It was one of the greatest shows I have seen in all my years.

Soon after the pack trip, all the temporary rangers except Jack Billings and me were laid off. I was kept on duty until October l, assigned by Irv Kerr to remeasure all the trails in the Giant Forest District. I did this by pushing a one-wheeled bicycle-type contrivance equipped with a cyclometer over the many miles of trails involved. Then, using the revolutions I had recorded, I spent almost a week computing and recording the results. Within a year or two all signs were replaced with these mileages.

September 30 was my last day on duty as temporary ranger in Sequoia National Park in 1935. I turned in my badge, collar ornaments, and miscellaneous NPS property items with which I was charged, and said my goodbyes. It was not a sad departure; I was young and footloose and looked eagerly ahead to my next venture.

However, I was not fancy free. There was the matter of the girl who had stolen my heart. Hilda lived in Exeter, and that evening I took her to a movie in Visalia, a few miles away. Afterwards, we returned to Exeter and then drove to an isolated spot atop an open, golden-carpeted hill that overlooked the town and part of the San Joaquin Valley. There we parked. It had seemed that the moon followed us and showered us with its beams everywhere we went that summer, and it was no different this night. The difference was that this was goodbye.

Ours had been a wonderful and wholesome relationship—warm, affectionate, and altogether innocent. The magic word "love" had never passed the lips of either one of us; we were not the kind to use that term loosely. I had long since sensed that the depth of her feeling for me did not match that of mine for her, and I couldn't have been in a worse position to try to change that equation. I was impecunious, had no profession or craft or trade, no job, and no prospect of one. I was still adrift in the Great Depression. Erstwhile poker player that I was, I knew a bad hand when I held one, so I had decided to throw it in. Before we left the hilltop I said to her, "I'm going to try to forget you."

She then answered in a voice full of feeling and wonder, "I'm not at all sure I want you to." This only made the parting more difficult.

We returned to the family home Hilda shared with her mother and sister, and I bedded down in the small guest cottage at the rear. Next morning after breakfast, that world came to an end when we bade each other a bittersweet farewell and I moved on to an uncertain future.

In Exile at Redwood Meadow

I had long wanted to explore the land south of the border, and now I had a little stake saved from my summer's earnings and was free to do so. While visiting my mother in Santa Monica, I became a beachcomber for six weeks while preparing for my trip and (unsuccessfully) seeking a travelling companion. Finally, in the romantic tradition of my adopted mentor, Richard Halliburton, on November 10, my twenty-sixth birthday, I took off alone on a vagabond exploration of much of Mexico. Adventure was my daily companion, highlighted by ascents of storied Popocatepetl (17,887 feet) and Ixtaccihuatl (17,342 feet). I rarely encountered an English-speaking person, but as I was proficient in the Spanish language and happy to sever all ties with my previously known world, that suited me.

Learning from a letter forwarded by my mother that I had done extremely well on the Border Patrol examination, I returned to the USA at the turn of the year and waited to be called for an interview in the near future. In the interim, I landed a job in mid-January as a riveter at the Consolidated Aircraft Corporation in San Diego, where I worked for three-and-a-half months in the wing section, helping build PBY Flying Boats for the U. S. Navy.

As time dragged on and no call came from the Border Patrol, I began to count the days when I could return to Sequoia. At the same time, my resolve to put Hilda out of my life melted and eventually caved in completely. She occupied my thoughts more and more, and I began to live for the day I could be with her again. I could not put the memories of the previous summer out of my mind and wanted nothing more of life than to repeat what we had known together. There had been some correspondence between us, but of an indifferent nature on her part. Nevertheless, I was hopeful.

Finally, the day came when I was in a position to bid goodbye to San Diego and head for what I hoped would be another summer of enchantment under the Big Trees. With joy in my heart, I reported for duty at Ash Mountain Head-quarters of Sequoia National Park on May 1, 1936; it was wonderful to be back. Perhaps a hundred people lived and worked in this serene little community in the canyon of the Middle Fork of the Kaweah River. Its name comes from the ash-covered, yucca-studded, granite battlement that towers some four hundred feet immediately above it, forming one wall of the canyon. The village itself lies on a bluff slightly above the river, at a point where the foothills sprawl briefly before zooming skyward. Below this point, the river careens and cascades its way down the beauty-laden canyon some twelve miles before spending its strength in the fertile but parched soil of the San Joaquin Valley. Above Ash Mountain, the Middle Fork snakes its way up, ever-upward into the snow-capped crest of the Great Western Divide. Through a lacework of oak leaves, ponderous Moro Rock and lovely Alta Peak form a magnificent backdrop for a vast cut in the canyon walls. To the north of Moro Rock, the venerable and majestic Sequoias, largest of living things, raise their shaggy manes on the Giant Forest plateau, 4,700 feet above the little village. Across the canyon to the south, Milk Ranch Peak leaps abruptly into the sky in gigantic grandeur.

It was like going home again. This was the human community at its best. I was immediately put to work at a variety of assignments that so absorbed my full attention day after day that seeing Hilda had to wait. I had no automobile, and there was no public transportation in or out of her little hometown, so I had caught a ride directly to Ash Mountain, thinking I would find a way to see her after I was settled on the job. I was patient because I anticipated that another glorious summer with her was just around the corner.

Meanwhile, I patrolled the park roads; controlled traffic; inspected trails; installed equipment in ranger cabins; helped move stock from winter quarters to working corrals; rode up the Middle Fork to check on the Redwood Meadow Ranger Station; transported powder and barley to road's end for a back-country trail crew; took instruction in horseshoeing and packing; collected and moved saddle and pack stock, equipment, and supplies from headquarters to trail head; performed office duty; answered letters of inquiry; and stood duty at the information station in Giant Forest. Three weeks passed with no time off; my thoughts were primarily concerned with the tasks I was performing, and I reveled in where I was doing it.

One day Captain Ford Spigelmyre, the chief ranger, called me into his office and asked, "Wallace, how would you like to have the Redwood Meadow station this summer?" Under the circumstances, this was a "when did you stop beating your wife?"-type of question if ever I heard one. Spig was canny that way, and I knew it. I had to be very careful. I replied, "That would be fine—sure, Redwood Meadow is a swell place." Although I tried to keep it out, there must have been some reluctance in my voice for Spig quickly and craftily asked, "But what station would you like best of all?"

Now I knew what assignment I desperately wanted, and he must have known too. Where else would any young pleasure-bent ranger want to go but back to Giant Forest

Village where the summer before I had had the best time of my life? Hadn't I looked forward all winter to a resumption of the friendships, the parties, the dances, the conveniences, and carefree life of this superb mountain resort? And wasn't the girl I was crazy about returning to her summer job there? To throw all this over for a lonely and remote outpost in the wilderness, many miles from the nearest person, was unthinkable.

I studied Spig at length before I answered. He sat behind his desk like a sphinx, a cockily tilted Stetson on his head. The gaze from his small, round eyes bored into me. I knew that I was engaged in a battle of wits with Spig, and that I had about as much chance of fooling that shrewd old gladiator as anyone in the then-current crop of young hopefuls had of overcoming Joe Louis.

Suddenly, the sphinx disappeared and his eyes became wells of understanding. Although I should have known from the experience of others that it would be fatal to my chances of getting there to let Spig know where I really wanted to go, I put everything into a desperate plea while his guard seemed to be down. "If you really want to know where I'd like to be stationed this summer—I'd like to go back to Giant Forest." He ended the interview with a non-committal, "Well, we'll see."

The next day, I cursed my gullibility and Spig's duplicity when he told me that he was sending me out to Redwood Meadow. He had dropped his guard all right, but only long enough to draw me in where he could land a blow that would really keep me out of mischief all that summer. He softened the blow a bit by beaming at me and saying, "Wallace, you know what the job is; go out there and do a good one. I don't care whatever else you do—just don't let me catch you at it."

I had to see Hilda before I moved out to Redwood Meadow. In another few weeks, she would be back at her old job in the post office in Giant Forest, seventeen miles by horseback from my newly assigned station. I could find reasons to ride into Giant Forest on official business or to pick up mail and supplies about twice a month, and on these occasions we could take up where we had left off the summer before. Better that than nothing at all, so I thought, driven by desperation into a state of naïveté.

The evening before I was to leave for Redwood Meadow, I borrowed a car and drove down to Exeter to see her. She was all that I remembered and seemed as responsive as ever. I was beside myself with delight. This was the girl I wanted. She had been in and out of my thoughts ever since we had parted in October, and at last here we were, together again. I was more captivated than ever. We went over to Terminus Beach, a secluded little resort on the Kaweah River where it broke out into the San Joaquin Valley, and danced the evening away. It was a wonderful time, and the memory of it is so poignant that one of the tunes we danced to—quite popular at the time—still haunts me: *The Lady in Blue.*

Hilda and I never danced together again, for that night the blow fell. She told me that the man with whom she had been going steady for some time in her hometown objected to her seeing me again this summer, and she had agreed not to do so. I was crushed. Stunned beyond words, I made no protest. It was not that I had not known about him, for I did; we had met once when he had come up to Giant Forest from the valley for a weekend. It was a strange situation, but their relationship did not seem to be particularly strong so I hadn't given it much weight. Somehow it penetrated my consciousness that I was in a no-win situation—how could I fight for her with both hands tied behind my back? I returned to my bachelor cabin at Ash Mountain and lay motionless, eyes wide open all night, staring into the darkness until the new day dawned. It was the worst night of my life, one in which I grew up a lot.

After a night completely bereft of sleep, I arose, dressed, and was ferried by another ranger to Moro Creek Corrals. There I saddled my horse, packed my mules, and rode the thirteen miles to Redwood Meadow, a desolate man. How could I know that day that I was riding into a new life that was as different as black from white from what I had known the summer before, one that was to be every bit its equal in its rich rewards?

Redwood Meadow is a lovely green gem that lies at an elevation of 6,400 feet on the western slope of the Great Western Divide between Granite and Cliff creeks, tributaries of the Middle Fork of the Kaweah River. About thirty acres in size, it sits in the midst of a modest-sized grove of *Sequoia-dendron giganteum* that is characterized by a mixture of ancient giants and prolific young growth. A little-travelled trail runs along its western fringe, and a snow-fed rivulet gurgles through its center. At the eastern edge, half-hidden in a clump of young Sequoia trees, sat a rustic one-room cabin that was now my home. The walls and the pitched roof were constructed with shakes, and the floor consisted of rough-hewn split timber, polished smooth by the years of wear. A small lean-to had been extended over the front, also roofed with shakes and supported by several five-inch uprights of peeled logs. Erected to serve some purpose in the distant past before this area became a part of the park, its character, together with the setting enhanced by isolation, gave it the ambiance of an earlier day when solitary mountain men pioneered the region. This is what I had fallen heir to.

Both the inside of the cabin and the surrounding yard were long-neglected. It took me two days to clean out the former and put the water system in working order and another day to shape up the yard. That was only a beginning; the entire district needed a lot of work. First, I had to put up the telephone line that ran toward Atwell Mill. I started early one morning and had fairly easy going as I dropped down the steep slope to the Cliff Creek crossing.

Repairing the breaks and stringing the line alone up the long, precipitous ridge that lies between Cliff Creek and Atwell Mill would have been hard work for a three-man crew. In all, I found five breaks in the line, and it was down in three other places from winter windfall. Hour after hour I struggled up that slope, pulling the line together and splicing the segments with connectors, fighting the brush that blocked my progress, tore my clothing, and jabbed my body. I forced my way through and up, dragging many feet of wire behind me, finally climbing the trees to which I fastened it. I paused only for a lunch I had packed, and stayed with it until the job was finished late in the afternoon. Then I still had to hike down the trail to Cliff Creek and climb back up on the other side. It was dusk by the time I reached my cabin, and I have never been more exhausted. I fell at once into bed and passed into oblivion. That experience remains vividly in my memory as the hardest day's work I have ever done.

The Middle Fork District for which I was responsible covered the entire western slope of the Great Western Divide, drained by the Kaweah watershed down to about 5,000 feet. It was as wondrous and hospitable a piece of terrain as exists in all the Sierra Nevada. It was my kingdom, and I came to love it dearly as I worked on the improvements that provided access and comfort to backcountry visitors. I began by cleaning up the nine campgrounds scattered within the district, painting old signs and placing about forty new ones, and repairing pasture fences. Another task involved clearing out overhead brush on horseback along the sixty-five miles of forest trails so that they could be safely ridden even on the darkest night.

My concern for the safety of trail riders in my district was not confined to terra firma. Although I forded it a number of times in May and June, the trail crossing of the Middle Fork of the Kaweah River was hazardous. The runoff of melting snow from the high country turned this stream into a swift-moving, tumbling torrent that gave me pause almost every time I had to cross it. I felt as though I was literally putting my life at risk and had to depend on the sure-footed strength of my saddle horse to get me through an adventure that was too scary for comfort. I even trembled for the safety of my pack animals as they carefully braced themselves and gingerly picked their way through the submerged boulders. Others had been doing this for years, so I couldn't back off. However, I

Middle Fork Ranger District

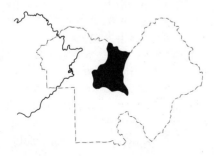

1. ELIZABETH PASS
   11,400'

2. LONE PINE MEADOW

3. TAMARACK LAKE
   9,215'

4. TRIPLE DIVIDE PEAK
   12,634'

5. LION LAKE
   11,005'

6. LION ROCK

7. MT. STEWART
   12,205'

8. HAMILTON LAKE
   8,235'

9. PRECIPICE LAKE

10. KAWEAH GAP
    10,700'

11. EAGLE SCOUT PEAK
    12,040'

12. MT. LIPPINCOTT
    12,265'

13. PINTO LAKE

14. BLACK ROCK PASS
    11,600'

15. TIMBER GAP
    9,511'

16. SAWTOOTH PASS
    11,700'

17. MINERAL KING
    7,831'

18. ALTA PEAK
    11,204'

19. ALTA MEADOW

20. BEARPAW CAMP
    7,800'

21. SUGAR BOWL DOME

22. LITTLE BEARPAW MEADOW

23. REDWOOD MEADOW R.S.
    6,400'

24. CASTLE ROCKS
    9,081'

25. ATWELL MILL R.S.
    6,445'

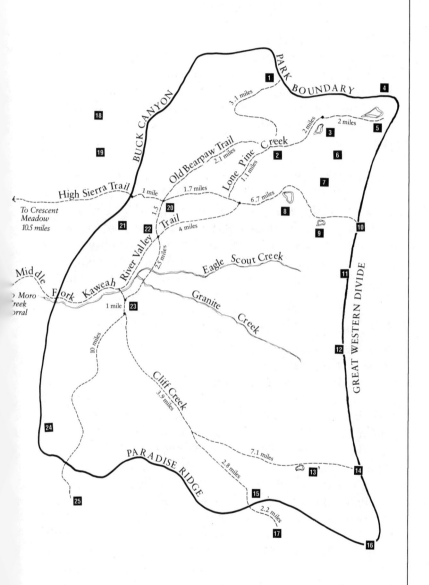

felt that this situation was a disaster waiting to happen, so I strongly recommended that the river be bridged at this point; some years later, it was.

Under my supervision CCC crews worked on the trails and improved campgrounds all that summer. I also kept a watchful eye on zealous fisherfolk. Most important of all, there were the visitors to be served—a total summer traffic of twelve hundred people and eight hundred fifty head of stock. This and other responsibilities required me to patrol by horseback a total of approximately fourteen hundred miles during four months of my reign. By the time visitation increased around the first of July, I had things in pretty good shape.

Acting as a trail guide for visiting groups was another of my responsibilities. Parties were generally no larger than five people, but there were two notable exceptions, both of which involved the Sierra Club. Even then this organization was prominent as a political force in the American conservation movement. One of its most important activities was conducting an "outing program" that dispatched its members in large groups to familiarize them with the wonders of the great outdoors, especially in the western United States. After seeing our great national heritage for themselves, members returned to their homes nationwide to preach the gospel of protection and preservation of outstanding scenic, recreational, and wilderness resources. As a result, the Sierra Club was treated with deference in Sequoia National Park, as well as in other similar areas. There was, however, a problem: how to minimize the impact of large numbers of people, horses, and mules in the sections traversed.

In the case of the first group that proposed to visit the Middle Fork District in July 1936, Superintendent White and Assistant Chief Ranger Kerr rode out to River Valley and met me. This valley, a pristine area that ranged for several miles along the Middle Fork of the Kaweah, far below the High Sierra Trail, was little travelled, and its potential for a quick recovery from a one-time large encampment made it a logical choice for a Sierra Club stopover. The next two days we searched for suitable sites for the one hundred eighty people who would be the district's guests the following month. Not only was a large, hospitable space required for sleeping and preparation of meals, but pasturage and drift fences for ninety head of stock also had to be considered. After the exact site had been pinned down, I was occupied at intervals for several weeks thereafter supervising the work of a CCC crew setting up hitching racks, drift fences, gates, and latrines.

On July 11, I met Allie Robinson's pack train of sixty mules and thirty horses at the suspension bridge on the High Sierra Trail above Hamilton Lake and escorted it to the River Valley campsite. It carried equipment and provision for the scores of hikers who came over Kaweah Gap from the Kern River watershed.

I remained with the Sierra Club encampment during their layover in River Valley to assist, inform, and guide as the occasion arose. It was an orderly group, one that paid strict attention to wilderness etiquette, and they left minimal evidence of their presence. What few scars were created were healed in good time by nature.

In early August, another wave of Sierra Club hikers, one hundred fifteen in all, came over Elizabeth Pass from Sequoia National Forest to the north and camped in Lonepine Meadow; I had spent the previous five days supervising a CCC crew in the preparation of a campsite for this invasion. This event remains memorable mainly for the confrontation I had with one of the hikers. I had been instructed by the chief ranger to make certain that they behaved themselves while in my area, so I had ridden up to meet them as they spilled over the pass like a swarm of locusts. Afire with the zeal of youth and dedicated to the protection of my wilderness, I carefully observed them as they passed me on the way to their camp. All was in order.

Or was it? At the tail end of the procession I spotted a straggler, a man about ten years older than I, who came jouncing jauntily down the trail swinging a pine staff that appeared to have been freshly broken from a live tree. That was a flagrant violation of park rules and regulations, so I

45

accosted him and without preliminaries proceeded to give him a sound lecture on park preservation.

During my harangue, he stood meekly with a sort of half-smile on his lips, and when I had finished he said, "But, Ranger, I took this staff from a down tree on the other side of the pass." That would be Forest Service land, which was administered under a different policy and was beyond my jurisdiction. Of course, this took the wind out of my sails, but he graciously saw to it that my embarrassment was quickly dissipated and thanked me for my conscientious concern. That night, when he arose to speak to the group at the club's campfire, I learned that this was Ansel Adams, a man already known to me by reputation as a leading conservationist as well as photographer.

There were other members in the group who also were well-known. For example, Francis Tappaan, a former football All-American end at USC, was the personable and competent leader, and William Colby, one of the founding fathers of the club, was present. Although Colby was a gentle and quiet-spoken man then well along in years, in my contact with him I detected a magnetism that explained in part the wilderness patriarch he had become.

Almost thirty-five years passed before I saw Ansel Adams again, on the occasion of a small reception at the Bancroft Library on the campus of the University of California at Berkeley, a function at which my wife and I were guests of Francis and Majorie Farquhar. Francis, editor of the *Sierra Club Bulletin* for twenty-two years, twice president of the Sierra Club, former president of the California Historical Society, and an eminent historian of the Sierra Nevada in his own right, had become a good friend of mine. Thus it was that Francis and his longtime friend Ansel Adams and I wound up in a threesome comparing a few notes.

During the course of our conversation I asked Ansel if he remembered the occasion of our first meeting at which I had lectured him on conservation. At first he smiled, then joined me in a hearty laugh about the incident. To this day, I am not entirely sure that Ansel Adams actually recalled the 1936 affair, but the obvious warmth and spontaneity of his reaction to my tale seemed proof that he did. But even if this were not so, you may be sure that Ansel Adams would react in a way he thought would make me comfortable, for he was that kind of a man—one of the most gracious I have ever met.

Although the traffic through my district, especially along the popular High Sierra Trail, kept me well occupied, my duties still required me more often than not to spend time at my station at Redwood Meadow. I had a number of good books to read and was not disturbed by having to go several days without seeing anyone. However, I enjoyed the company of my friends too. Attracted by my situation, my guests that summer were frequent; we enjoyed the best of times, both at the cabin and on the trail.

Among those I invited were Dick Simmons and Nora, the girl he later married. Dick was an intimate friend, a buddy from the days when we eked out a living parking cars in the auto parks of Los Angeles for twenty-five cents an hour. Dick and Nora were with me for a week. Most of that time we rode the trails on patrol. Once Assistant Chief Ranger Kerr rode with us, and we camped together at Tamarack Lake. We also enjoyed a couple of days at the station, a delightful change of pace. Both have often told me that this was the most memorable week of their lives.*

Overwhelmed though all my visitors were that summer by their experience in my mountain Utopia, the impact of the environment and the life I led had an even greater effect on me. I was a changed man. This can be illustrated no better than by what happened when, early in August, I rode into the Wolverton Corrals for only the second time that summer to pick up mail and supplies. I was met at the corrals by Dave Bristow, my cabinmate of the previous summer, a friend whom I greatly admired. We had just settled ourselves in the

---

*Some years later, Dick made it big in the movies and TV where he became best known as the star of the popular television series, "Sergeant Preston of the Yukon." Today we are practically neighbors, living only fifteen minutes apart, keeping invigorated a friendship that has endured since 1933.

ALONG THE HIGH SIERRA TRAIL NEAR BEARPAW CAMP

THE ANGEL'S WING ABOVE HAMILTON LAKE

pickup truck to drive to the village, where I would put up during my short stay, when he turned to me and said, "Wally, there is something that I should tell you; I have been seeing a lot of Hilda this summer."

I was surprised. This was the guy who, about midway into the summer before, had gone out of his way to keep the romance between Hilda and me alive and well. Now, a year later, Dave had taken my place. Remarkably, I accepted this information without a twinge of regret. Not that I had forgotten Hilda—indeed the memory was fond—but she now belonged to a world that I had successfully left behind. To put Dave at ease, I told him so and wished him well.

Notable among the visitors to my district during the course of the summer was Mrs. Herbert Hoover. When I dropped by her camp one day at Bearpaw Meadow Campground, I saw that she was busy just outside her tent. I wanted to tell her that I was a great admirer of her husband, the only President in the history of our nation who refused to take any pay for serving his country as its Chief Executive, but I chose not to intrude on her privacy.

Human companions came and went, but there were four-footed friends who shared my life daily throughout the summer, those who were steadfast and special. One was as unique an animal as I have ever known. Her name was Gracie—a small white mule, almost petite. Of indeterminate age, she was far past her prime, and carried herself with dignity; nothing ruffled or hurried her. You got the impression that she had seen it all and was circumspectly disdainful of those of us who had not yet matured. Gracie was my reserve pack animal, and I usually took her with me on short patrols where there were no heavy loads to carry. Gentle and well-behaved, the only time she objected to my demands was when I was obviously making such a fool of myself that she could no longer idly bear it. Not only was she wise, she was smart—the only one of the equine breed that I have known who could unlatch a gate. My cabin was inside the fenced-in pasturage of the meadow, and sometimes on my return from a two- or three-day patrol, I would turn Gracie loose so she could go ahead and open the gate for us. It was a marvel to watch that little white-whiskered head nuzzle the latch up and push open the gate, then trot daintily on to the cabin and wait patiently to be relieved of the burden she was carrying.

My other pack animal could be ridden in a pinch, but she was my primary beast of burden. She was an ordinary bay mare whose name escapes me now, but I do remember that she discharged her duties faithfully and well. And then, to round out the trio of my four-footed charges, there was Budge, my saddle horse. There has been no other horse in my life quite as dear to me.

To look at Budge you would not suspect that he was something special. Well into the middle years of life, he conducted himself with a dignity befitting his age. He was of average size. Even his color was run-of-the-mill—just plain black. Honesty precludes me from saying, in an effort to glamorize him, that his coat shimmered in the sun. It didn't; he would strike a stranger as just another horse. Budge and I were close companions, roaming together over hundreds of miles of trail through some of the most magnificent terrain in the West. He really was my partner, for I rarely made a patrol without him.

Budge was a trail-smart veteran who was as sure-footed in the mountains as any of its undomesticated four-legged inhabitants. On occasion he was not above subtly questioning my authority with a snort of disgust and a turn of the head, showing disdain as I directed him to do something that he felt was nothing less than stupid. But he tolerated me, and in time we came to share a secret that bound us together in a kinship that I'd like to tell you about, now that Budge is no doubt happily grazing in a lush meadow in horse heaven and I no longer need answer to any human being for certain actions of my past.

It is extremely rare to find in the High Sierra a level

stretch of trail without twists and turns where a horse may be turned loose at full speed for several hundred yards. One I know lies along the High Sierra Trail just beyond Bearpaw Meadow Camp, some twelve miles east of its western terminus at Crescent Meadow on the Giant Forest Plateau. Here, at an elevation of some 8,000 feet, the trail is not only level and relatively free of rocks, but it is somewhat wider than normal, a good six feet. At this point, as one faces eastward, a precipitous mountainside rises abruptly from the trail on the left. It is covered with fir and aspen and multicolored wildflowers, all of which cling precariously to the boulder-studded slope as it reaches for the generally faultless blue sky.

On the right, the trail-edge breaks off abruptly in a sheer plunge of a thousand feet or more to River Valley below, part of a region called Valhalla because of its mythic beauty. Rising on the far side above this narrow valley—really a canyon—are a series of great granite shields that were carved and polished in a glacial age and now shine white and monstrous as they leap toward the summit of the Great Western Divide.

It was here that Budge and I found that we were kindred spirits. I had no doubt about my own, for in my mid-twenties, animated by a deep sense of adventure, there was hardly a risk I would not take to experience the unbounded exhilaration that lifted me above ordinary mortals. Hence it was that each time we came to this stretch without a pack animal in tow, I would give Budge a hard kick in the ribs and then let nature take its course. He inevitably responded with a fire and a speed that were superb, a worthy descendant of his forbear in classical mythology. Considered sensibly, this adventure was irrational. A misstep or a stumble by Budge could easily have catapulted us both over the edge of the trail into space from which there would be no return.

But each time we had the chance, off we sped at breakneck pace, the wind whipping through Budge's mane and whistling around my ears. We were so close to the edge that, sitting in my saddle, I could see nothing to my right except the yawning void below and the great granite battlements rising above it across the way. The straining, surging animal life under me, the smooth-flowing speed, and the sensation of having left the earth to fly across the Sierra skies was no less than being borne aloft on the wings of Pegasus.

When we were at home, it was my custom occasionally to check on my quadruped companions to assure myself that all was well. One day, midway through a golden Sierra afternoon, I stepped out of my ramshackle cabin and spotted Gracie and the horses at the upper end of the meadow, perhaps sixty yards away. They were not alone. Rounding out as strange a tableau as one could chance to see was a well-antlered buck and a doe of the California mule deer species, as well as a nearly full-grown American black bear. They were grouped within a circle about fifty feet in diameter, all intent on filling their stomachs with the succulent forage that carpeted the meadow. Oblivious to all else, they moved at random, but always with care not to disturb one another. It was a rare and beautiful sight. What a pity, I thought, that disparate elements of the human race cannot accommodate one another in a similar manner.

The black bear was no novelty to me. Our paths rarely crossed, but when they did, we managed to give each other a wide berth. I was satisfied with merely a passing acquaintance, but one night one of them carried our relationship a bit too far—or better put, brought it too close. I had returned late in the afternoon from an exhausting, fun- and work-filled three-day excursion to Giant Forest and Visalia for mail and supplies. Too tired to think of anything else, I unsaddled and unpacked my stock, turned them loose, and carried my provisions inside. Too weary to move them inside the cabin, I left standing at the foot of the nearest tree two sacks of barley still strapped in their slings. The grain was intended to supplement the grassy diet of my stock. I removed my outer garments and boots and burrowed into my sleeping bag just as the sun was setting.

Except during stormy weather, I always slept outside. My

bed was a pallet of fir needles spread under a canopy of the overarching limbs of a youthful Sequoia that filtered beams of the moon and allowed just enough stars to sparkle through to induce a bewitched sleep. But something awakened me in the middle of that particular night, a nervous and persistent sound, a soft, almost-silent shuffle. It came from near the head of my bed, which abutted one of the trees against whose bole I had a few hours before hastily set my sacks of the barley. I raised up in my sleeping bag and turned my head in the direction of the sound; at the same time, a medium-sized black bear swiveled its head toward me, curious as to what was disturbing the even tenor of its nocturnal foray. One of its arms embraced a sack of barley, and its other paw was dipped into the sack, caught in the act like a child with its hand in a forbidden cookie jar.

For a second or so we stared at each other, eyeball to eyeball, only about ten inches separating us. I reacted first and took the offensive. I let out a silence-shattering war-whoop rendered with the maximum capacity of my lungs, then retired discreetly, immediately, and completely into the recesses of my sleeping bag.

The bear, more frightened than I, could not get away fast enough from this terrible apparition that had surprised it in its thievery and shaken its composure. It dropped its plunder and took off as though shot from a cannon; it let nothing stand in its way. For what seemed forever, I could hear it crashing through the forest, breaking off limbs and scurrying over windfalls in its haste to put a great distance between itself and me. I approved of his hasty retreat, but I slept no more that night. Neither did I ever again, in my years in the mountains, leave barley exposed to tempt an omnivorous animal.

There were probably a dozen or so bear around Bearpaw Meadow, Redwood Meadow, and along the Middle Fork. Other wildlife also flourished in the district. Deer were numerous and in good shape; I spotted a six-point buck several times in Lonepine Meadow. Grouse did well in all sections, and there were perhaps ten well-scattered coveys of mountain quail. Rattlesnakes were plentiful in River Valley, and there were a few around Bearpaw Meadow. Once or twice a month I would spot the silvery flash of a beautiful Columbia grey squirrel in the vicinity of Redwood Meadow. I saw only one coyote all summer, but there was no lack of marmots in the higher elevations.

Although it excites and thrills most everyone to encounter wildlife in the mountains, fishing offers an even greater attraction. Within the Middle Fork District, Hamilton Lake furnished the best fishing. No matter how many trout were taken from this lake, many more remained; I saw some caught that were fourteen inches long and others in the water that would measure eighteen inches. Tamarack Lake also provided good fishing, while easily accessible Cliff Creek, the most heavily fished of all streams, was only fair.

In regard to weather, the Sierra Nevada enjoys a reputation as the most hospitable mountain range in the world. John Muir called it "The Range of Light." Nonetheless it has enough diversity, even in the summer, to ward off monotony. According to my diary, during the 1936 season in the Middle Fork District, skies were clear sixty percent of the time, partly cloudy twenty percent and cloudy twenty percent. A cold rain fell on May 28, followed by two inches of snow that night. On June 3, it snowed heavily all day at the ranger station, with a six-inch accumulation. Snow fell as late as July 10, and the first frost of fall occurred on September fourth. There was rain on twenty-three days, accompanied by thunderstorms on fifteen. While I camped in the River Valley on July 10, an earthquake struck about eight P.M., creating a large avalanche of rock down the slope across the river, opposite from where I watched.

My tenure at Redwood Meadow ended late in September. Between the eleventh and the twenty-third of that month, I pushed a cyclometer over every mile of maintained trail in the Middle Fork District—one hundred, to be exact—to provide accuracy for the new signs being fashioned at headquarters,

RANGER WALLACE AT THE REDWOOD MEADOW
RANGER STATION

ON PATROL WITH BUDGE AND GRACIE

as had been the case with my survey on the Giant Forest Plateau just a year before. Although this was a much more demanding chore, including as it did rugged trails and mountain passes more than 10,000 feet in elevation (Elizabeth Pass, Kaweah Gap, and Black Rock Pass), I was in great shape after four months of active, outdoor mountain life and considered it a fitting way to end my 1936 stay.

I had thought all summer of climbing Triple Divide Peak, and on September 17, I finally found a good chance to do so. I had propelled my cyclometer all the way up the Lone Pine Creek trail to its head at Lion Lake, and there, looming just above me, was Triple Divide Peak in all its rugged glory. So I left my cyclometer at the lake and made my way to the summit. It was a steep climb, but hazardous only in one stretch where I had to pick my way cautiously up a knife-like ridge near the top where there was nothing but a lot of thin air on both sides. The view from Triple Divide, as its name implies, encompasses three of the most spectacular watersheds in the Sierra Nevada: the Kings, the Kern, and the Kaweah. The view took my breath away, more so than did the climb itself. This little adventure was a fitting finale to a marvelous sojourn in the backcountry of the Middle Fork of the Kaweah.

On September 23, I closed the Redwood Meadow Station and rode into Wolverton Corrals, where I parted company with my faithful four-footed companions. In a sharp bit of irony, I was assigned to the information station in Giant Forest the last week of the month, to close out my tour of duty on September thirtieth. Spig had finally granted my wish to return to Giant Forest, but it was too little, too late. In the intervening four months my life had changed, and I found the scenes of yesteryear a bit dull. The summer of 1936, in giving me a new life of such challenging and wonderful dimensions, would be hard to equal.

4

Return to Eden

Again adrift with no job and still without word from Border Patrol authority, I struck out for Berkeley to visit Ralph Wise and his family. Ralph had moved there to work for his cousin Lloyd, one of the Bay Area's largest Oldsmobile dealers; and I spent some of my summer's earnings to buy a used car from Ralph. This put me back on wheels for the first time in three years. I also spent a weekend with Ned Munn, who was now living in Berkeley. He had married and was working in a federal office in San Francisco.

I then drove up through the magnificent redwood forest of northern California and on to Crater Lake and finally to Burns on the high desert of eastern Oregon. In Burns I renewed friendships with some of those I had worked with while helping build the lumber mill there, installing its machinery, and then handling lumber in the shipping department after the mill went into operation in the spring of 1930.

Upon returning to California, I stopped at the prestigious Ahwanee Hotel in Yosemite Valley to seek employment for the winter. The personnel manager expressed regrets that he was already fully staffed, but strongly recommended that I try Death Valley. I took his advice and wound up in November as the front-desk clerk at the Amargosa Hotel in Death Valley Junction. When a severe winter set in after the first of the year and tourist travel evaporated, I was transferred to Death Valley proper, where I was put to work at all kinds of tasks for the Pacific Coast Borax Company. For a time I was room clerk at the Furnace Creek Camp, then assistant stone-mason, narrow-gauge railway section hand, general handy man, and hard rock miner. Finally, when business picked up again, I was reinstalled as room clerk and asked to help out in the company store. On several occasions I was loaned to Tanner Tours as a chauffeur-guide to drive tourists around the valley. Death Valley National Monument had been established only a few years before, under the administration of Colonel White. It was here that I met Ranger Jack Nealis, who later transferred to Sequoia and became a close friend and associate.

All in all, my sojourn of more than four months in Death Valley and environs was broadening and delightful, leavened as it was by off-duty associations with the young, unattached socialites and Hollywood starlets who made the Furnace Creek Inn their winter hideout. Nevertheless, when the summer heat set in, I was ready to leave and return to Sequoia National Park for my third season as a temporary ranger.

I reported for duty on May 5, 1937. For almost two weeks I filled in at the checking station at the entrance to the park, performed chores in the chief ranger's office, made a few automobile patrols, got my stock and equipment together at the Ash Mountain Corrals and transferred everything to the Moro Creek Corrals, and finally rode out to Redwood Meadow Ranger Station and back to check on the need for repairs and replacements. Then, on May 17, I rode out to Redwood Meadow with my equipment and supplies to take up residence for the summer. Although the novelty of the assignment had worn off a bit because of my experiences of the previous summer, it was great to be back at my old stand. I anticipated another marvelous summer.

I had occupied the station only eight days when I rode back down the Middle Fork to Moro Rock Corrals. The next day (May 27), Henry Schmidt and I again drove to Fresno, this time to take the U.S. Civil Service Examination for park ranger. It had been almost two years since we had taken the Border Patrol exam, and we were both still without permanent employment. This exam was just another stone we could not leave unturned in our efforts to get some kind of job security. Both of us were much taken with the life of a park ranger as we had experienced it as temporaries, so a shot at that was most welcome. But Fate held the hole card as to the direction it would point each of us and was not yet ready to reveal it. The next day I rode back to Redwood Meadow to resume in earnest my duties for the summer.

To begin with, there was the task of shaping up the cabin and grounds. After that there were patrols to be made over district trails and up into the high passes to ascertain snow conditions and the maintenance required to repair winter storm damage. Later, when several CCC crews were placed at my disposal, I was responsible for overseeing their work. A ten-man crew constructed a new telephone line from Redwood Meadow to hook up with the High Sierra line in River Valley, installed a new cable at the suspension bridge above Hamilton Lake, and rolled up the abandoned telephone line over Kaweah Gap. This same crew also put into good shape the Old Bearpaw Trail, making practicable the traverse that climbed directly from a point on Lonepine Creek on the Elizabeth Pass trail to Bearpaw Camp. This was a skyline path that presented a spectacular close-up view of the great granite shields of the Great Western Divide and the deep Middle Fork Canyon far below.

There was also a smaller crew of three CCC enrollees that I kept busy for a month or so at Redwood Meadow rolling up all the old wire in the pasture and vicinity and putting up a new wire fence. They also installed foot logs at Granite Creek and Eagle Scout Creek on the River Valley Cutoff and at Cliff Creek on the Atwell Mill Trail. This crew also improved the forage in the pasture at Redwood Meadow by eradicating the skunk cabbage and coneflowers that were threatening to take over.

At the same time I continued to make the patrols that were necessary to contact visitors to protect them as well as the park, to improve campgrounds, and to keep fishermen in line. In short, my responsibilities and experiences during this summer of 1937 matched those of the previous summer so well that to recite them again here would be repetitious.

My records show that I took a total of six days off that summer: none at the ranger station, all on personal business outside the park. Although I rode more than seven hundred miles on patrol, I still put in fifteen days on duty at my ranger station. These were used to assist passersby, do my laundry, chop firewood, shoe my horses and mule, write reports, and entertain any guests who happened to be on hand. Although this sounds innocuous—and generally was—I once had a close call just a dozen steps from my cabin door.

I was shoeing Budge and had one of his rear hooves clamped between my knees. It is no picnic to shoe a horse or mule even in the best of circumstances, but when an animal gets nervous, there can be hell to pay. I don't know what disturbed Budge; after all, he had it pretty easy: I was holding up half his rear end while he leaned his weight on me as I tacked on a shoe. Suddenly Budge withdrew his foot with such force that I could not hold it, and a jutting nail, still remaining to be bent over the hoof, tore open my trousers from near the groin to below the knee. I missed having my leg ripped open by a matter of an inch or so. Budge was a gentle horse, so I had not taken the precaution of securing his leg by roping it in a sling. At any rate, add that to the hazards confronting not only a ranger in the backcountry, but all who frequent mountainous areas, either afoot or on horseback.

On June 17, Assistant Chief Ranger Kerr and Park Architect Harold Fowler arrived at Redwood Meadow Ranger Station. The next day the three of us chose the site for a new cabin to be built along the trail on the western edge of the meadow. Irv

Kerr remained a week, riding with me on patrols to various parts of the district, and then together we rode into the Wolverton Corrals. I then took off for southern California for two days on a mission that I will discuss later.

All parts of my district were so closely accessible that I rarely had to make an overnight camp. Although the station itself was isolated, I was seldom lonely. As in the previous summer, friends came and went with considerable frequency. They were my guests at Redwood Meadow where I was pleased to introduce them to an alluring new way of life. I did not neglect my responsibilities, but I had everything so well organized that I was able to have my cake and eat it too, a perfect situation where stimulating work and the companionship of fine friends filled my days and nights in a world so wonderful that one must have lived in it to believe it.

Among those whom I invited to visit me were Florence and Helen, girls I had met in Death Valley and later saw again when they invited me to a theater party in Los Angeles. They were a lively, fun-loving pair, and I was sure we could have a good time together. Helen asked if her friend Emil could come along. Of course I had no objection; this would round out things nicely. Besides, he was a great fisherman and could keep us supplied with delicious trout, only a few hours out of nearby Sierra streams. I rode into Wolverton to meet them on July 11—the day that, entirely unsuspected by me, initiated a new phase in my life.

Always one to appreciate a pretty face and a fine feminine figure, I had been much impressed with the beauty and glamour of the lovely blonde of my short Death Valley and Los Angeles acquaintance. I had been, however, in no way moved off an even keel. After Hilda, girls had lost their priority in my life. When I met Florence that day in Giant Forest, I saw her in a different light than before. I became interested, real interested. It is hard to say whether this was due to the way she fit into the ambiance of the Giant Forest I loved so dearly, or whether at last cosmic forces were at work to compel me to do my part to keep the world going around. Whatever the reason, I began to lose my head; and I was not the only one.

The next day matters accelerated. Early in the morning the four of us rode out of the Wolverton Corrals along the Wolverton Cutoff Trail. This route offered an easy grade up and through the magnificent coniferous forest of the Giant Forest Plateau, a forest that John Muir called the finest in the world, past thickets of incense cedar, through clumps of fir and pine, and under those towering and majestic giants, the Sequoias. We struck the Alta Trail, turned onto it, and began to climb through blossoming manzanita and ceanothus, brilliant green meadows sparkling in the crisp air and bright sunshine, and past gardens of varicolored wild-flowers scattered along the sunny slopes.

At Panther Gap we topped the ridge. The Great Western Divide with its magnificent array of sawtooth peaks beckoned us toward their granite slopes, still splotched with last winter's snows. At the bottom of the deep canyon below us, the Kaweah River roared its foaming-white course over gigantic boulders and down leaping cataracts.

After a ride that was filled with ever-changing and always-fascinating panoramas, we suddenly emerged from a dense forest and came into Redwood Meadow, lush with sweet green grass and gurgling with running water from melting snow. The sun projected long fingers of shade as it lowered in the West, and in its last reflected blaze of golden glory, the orange trunks of the Sequoias at the edge of the meadow became pillars of fire topped with blue-green. On the fringe and half-hidden in a clump of young Sequoias sat the little rustic cabin that was my mountain home.

It had been a day no dream could match. As Florence and I rode along hour after hour, how could I escape the romance of person and place that combined to overwhelm me? I could not, and I did not. There was no way to turn: we were both in beyond our depth.

One afternoon was especially memorable. That morning I had ridden over to Eagle Scout Creek about three miles away to supervise the laying of foot logs so hikers could cross the stream, and had returned to the station for lunch. Afterwards, Florence and I saddled up and headed for Raspberry

Meadow. It lay perhaps half a mile up a trail—then obscure and now probably totally obliterated—that rose steeply up the ridge to the south of Granite Creek. It was a spot so secluded that I know of only one person who had ever been there: the old-timer who told me about it.

It was a small meadow, hardly two hundred feet in diameter, an emerald gem of the purest hue, stippled lavishly with countless multicolored wildflowers at the height of their blossom time. A break in the forest on one side opened up a view of the peaks of the Great Western Divide with their snow fields so close that it seemed one could reach out and touch them. On the other three sides, lesser and closer peaks arose to enclose the meadow in their embrace. I see it still: remote, untouched, ethereal, small enough to be intimate, a romantic hideaway unsurpassed in its beauty and ambiance. For several hours one afternoon it belonged to me and my lady love, wherein we shared the ultimate romance that can be experienced on a spiritual plane.

The next morning I took off alone for Bearpaw Camp on the High Sierra Trail. I had learned that Chief Ranger Spigelmyre and two others, Homer Hardin, assistant park maintenance chief and Wesley Loverin, a temporary ranger serving as packer, were due in my district that day on an inspection trip in the backcountry. Either outbound or inbound, they were to stop at Redwood Meadow, but I could not learn which way they planned it. With a cabin full of guests and all the appearance (and reality) of grand and glorious revelry, I could ill afford to have the chief come my way that day. After all, he was the man who told me the year before, "I don't care what you do out there, just don't let me catch you at it." So, acting on this warning, I proposed to meet the party at Bearpaw and, if necessary, convince them to continue on to Hamilton Lake and over Kaweah Gap to the Kern District, stopping by Redwood Meadow on the way back. This appeared to be their plan anyway, but to make certain they would not surprise me, I accompanied them all the way to Hamilton Lake before I left them and returned to Redwood Meadow after a day-long, seventeen-mile ride.

The week that Florence and Helen and Emil had arranged to spend with me was nearing its conclusion with a rapidity that alarmed us all. Only two days remained before it would be time to escort them back to Giant Forest, and the ride I most wanted them to experience had yet to be made. So the very next day, after I had seen the chief's party on its way, we saddled up and made as lovely and breathtaking a circuit as can be made in the High Sierra on the back of a horse. About four miles after leaving Redwood Meadow, we came to the Middle Fork of the Kaweah and followed it up through River Valley, an idyllic region boasting a carpet of many-hued wildflowers; graceful firs; and precipitous, heaven-reaching walls. At its upper end the trail switchbacked up to the High Sierra Trail, where it passed under the Angel's Wing and emerged at Hamilton Lake.

Beyond Hamilton Lake the trail ascended to Precipice Lake. This is a small body of melted snow with deep, blue-green depths, at the base of a huge granite battlement. One of the most alluring sights in the Sierra Nevada, it is unique and mesmerizing. From there, the trail leveled off, winding through a rock garden of dainty alpine flowers endowed with great beauty by nature to compensate for the shortness of their lives. Just beyond that we topped off at Kaweah Gap, at 10,700 feet above sea level, a pass on the Great Western Divide that separates the watersheds of the Kern and Kaweah rivers. Dead ahead lay the broad sweep of the Big Arroyo, above which the Black and Red Kaweahs reach high into the sky, while in the distance beyond Skyparlor Meadow and the declivity of the Kern Canyon looms the crest of the Sierra Nevada. We tarried there a while, trying to make it a part of our being, then turned back.

Of all the memorable moments that day, why one stands out above all others is hard to say. Perhaps it was that everything conjoined at that particular point to create an exaltation that lifted me among the gods. It struck me as we descended the trail just below Precipice Lake. Florence and I were leading our horses, to give them a break. There she was, just a few steps ahead of me, the queen of my heart, the one person for whom I considered the world well lost. There we walked together, no others in sight, surrounded by the finest that nature affords, in the region dearest to my heart, just the two of us in a world apart. To complete the illusion, far, far down the western horizon in another world, across lowering ranges and ridges, lay the brown blanket of summer-heat haze that hid the great San Joaquin Valley. More than half a century later the thought of it stirs me still.

Eventually I came down to earth, and we returned to Redwood Meadow by way of Bearpaw Camp. This is the tented tourist accommodation that occupies a magnificent site overlooking River Valley and the monstrous granite battlements that rise above it to form part of the backbone of the Great Western Divide. (The trail just east of the camp for several miles is my favorite in all the mountains of the world that I have known.) It was a long, hard day: twenty-six miles up and down high mountain trails where every step required a delicate balance between alertness to danger and an immersion in beauty.

Now only one day remained before I was to take Florence and Helen and Emil into Wolverton Corrals, and we made the most of it. It was a fitting windup to a week of trail rides, fish fries, jokes and laughter, and romancing under the moon. The sadness of goodbyes at Giant Forest the next day was tempered by the thought that we would soon be seeing each other again.

How soon I didn't know, but things were looking up. Just two years after taking the Border Patrol exam, I had been notified to appear on June 25 for a personal interview in West Los Angeles. At last, here was the next step. I was glad it hadn't come sooner, for I would not have wanted to miss my life in Redwood Meadow and Death Valley. In fact, when the call came, it was so far from my mind that I was startled. But finally, here was a chance for that permanent job and a stable life that I had been seeking for ten years. So I rode into Giant Forest, took two days off, and appeared as requested.

There were three or four on the board who questioned me. One was the Chief Patrol Inspector of the Imperial Valley detachment of the U.S. Immigration Border Patrol; he would be my boss if I could convince them I was the kind of man they wanted. They put me at ease right from the start, and their questions were penetrating, relevant, and fair. The queries involved such matters as career aspirations and scenarios where good judgement had to be exercised, especially in conflicts between law and the preservation of life. I was closeted with them for perhaps an hour and departed confident that I had made the right impression, although they were noncommittal.

Late in July, not many days after the departure of the Los Angeles trio, I received notice of my selection for one of approximately thirty-five vacancies in the U.S. Immigration Border Patrol. No date for reporting was mentioned, but I thought it only fair to notify the chief ranger at once about what had developed. Of course he knew about the interview a month previously. As he should have, Spig arranged to have me replaced. I took the new man out to Redwood Meadow on July 31, spent the next day explaining to him his responsibilities, and on August 2 left my station at Redwood Meadow for good to report for duty at Ash Mountain.

There was no sadness attached to my departure from the post that had been a wonderful way station in my life, because too much exciting and new awaited me just ahead. Nevertheless, Redwood Meadow had given me in two summers as much of what I consider the finer things of life as most people come by in a lifetime.

Unbeknownst to me there remained a loose end to tie up, one that had its origin in the district from which I had just departed. Clarence Fry, my predecessor at Redwood Meadow, and I had been summoned to appear as witnesses for the federal government in a mining case then before the General Land Office in Sacramento. This involved a molybdenum claim near Tamarack Lake that had been initiated prior to that section being brought within the boundaries of the park. Some time before, the superintendent, having learned that the two claimants proposed to visit the site, had dispatched me, armed with a .38 Smith and Wesson on my hip, to keep an eye on them and prevent any further despoliation of the area. This I had done without any problem developing between me and the claimants. They were reasonable men. My testimony, for whatever it was worth, was sought. So it happened that on August 4 the three of us flew from Visalia to Sacramento and back in a four-place private plane to testify. It was an interesting experience; the most absorbing part of it for me was being in the air several hours each way, having flown only twice before and then only for a few minutes each.

As we approached the Visalia Airport on our return, Colonel White took over the controls from Sol Sweet, our pilot. The colonel was a bit of a flyer and wanted to make the landing. I had no problem with this, but Clarence Fry became extremely nervous. As the plane settled down and the ground flew up, Clarence, in great agitation, looked over the side as if trying to find a soft part of the earth on which to fall when the plane crashed, fidgeting all the while we descended. It didn't help his nerves any when the colonel overshot the field on his first attempt to land. I began to wonder a bit myself, but on the second try, the colonel set us down safely.

Within a few days, I received a letter from Washington requesting me to remain where I was, but to be prepared to report to El Paso on short notice between August 16 and September first. So the chief ranger kept me at Ash Mountain Headquarters, where I occasionally helped out in his office, but for the most part, I filled in at the park entrance checking station. Finally, the call came on August 21 to report at the Border Patrol Training School in El Paso, Texas, on September first. I then formally resigned my temporary ranger position and left the park. Those wonderful days when I was privileged to serve in Sequoia National Park as a temporary ranger had ended.

On Duty at Ash Mountain Checking Station

Once Upon a Happy Time in Three Rivers
(Florence and Gordon)

5

Back Home Again

Two years and four months later, I came back. The intervening period had been tempestuous and troublesome. Upon
completion of the Border Patrol Training School in late
November 1937, I was assigned to duty in the Imperial Valley
of California, stationed successively at El Centro, Brawley,
and Indio. Florence and I were married in April 1938, and she
fell critically ill two weeks later. Her life was saved only by
the new wonder drug, penicillin. We were so overwhelmed by
hospital and doctor bills from the very beginning that we had
to buy groceries on credit to put food on the table. Then
marital problems developed and grew alarmingly serious. The
marriage was in deep trouble.

In the meantime, I became unhappy with my life in the
Border Patrol. It had not turned out to be the career I sought,
so I decided in 1939 to try for a lateral transfer from the
Immigration and Naturalization Service to the National Park
Service. To do this, I had to find a job in one agency and a
release from the other. For a change, fortune smiled on me.

Two permanent ranger positions opened up in Sequoia National Park about this time, and I began campaigning for one of them. The superintendent and assistant superintendent were glad to have me back on a permanent basis, but this still depended on an official release from the Washington office of the Immigration and Naturalization Service. This eventually came through, and I went on duty at Ash Mountain Headquarters on the first day of 1940 as a member of the permanent ranger staff.

It was wonderful to be back in this serene and scenic environment, and in no time at all I regained a peace of mind and contentment that had been lacking in my life for a long time. It was as if I had been cast on a beautiful island, isolated from all troubles of the past.

There was no government housing available to me in the Ash Mountain Village, so I found a place in Three Rivers—a small but comfortable bungalow along the main highway leading into the park several miles away. It would do fine for the three of us (a son had been born four months before) until we could get a place at Ash Mountain. As things turned out, a move to Ash Mountain became academic. The first week of May Florence took our baby son and returned to her parental home. She never came back. I was devastated.

Within six weeks my problems came perilously close to being solved with frightful finality. I now lived in a bachelor cabin at Ash Mountain where I was regularly assigned to duty at the entrance checking station. The headquarters and homes of this little village rested on a bluff just above the Middle Fork of the Kaweah. At this spot, the river boasted a beautiful and alluring natural swimming hole; I had spent many idyllic leisure hours in its waters and on its banks in August of 1937 while awaiting orders to report to El Paso. I loved to swim, particularly here. Without a family to care for in my off-duty time, my need for exercise turned me toward the river.

There were two others likewise drawn to test the waters. One was Howard Liddell, Jr., the son of the park's purchasing agent, and the other was Daniel J. (Jim) Tobin, Jr., son of Sequoia's assistant superintendent. Both were about eighteen at the time, while I was thirty. I knew them well; we were all members of a tightly knit National Park Service family who lived close together in modest homes clustered around park headquarters. During their teen-age years I often waved them past the checking station as the school bus bore them down the road to Woodlake where they attended high school. Howard was a tall, slender, rather handsome, soft-spoken youth, while Jim, somewhat shorter, was robust and invariably cheerful. I considered them to be good, well-bred boys, and I like them both.

One afternoon in the middle of June the three of us scurried down the trail that dropped precipitously from the headquarters area down the side of the canyon to the river's edge. We were eager to have our first swim of the year. But we found the waters of our pool, so gentle and caressing in midsummer, now in frightening flood from the run-off of melting snow. A swim was out of the question, but, after a careful survey of the situation, I decided we could still salvage a piece of the action.

A ledge of granite, about a foot wide, stretched across the river and formed a natural dam that backed up the waters of our pool. Later in the year, after the melting snow from above had run off, water flowed lazily over the dam at a depth of barely an inch or so, but it now coursed strongly and swiftly over this restraining obstacle at a depth of about sixteen inches. Only four or five feet below the top of the dam, the falling water sought its level in another fast-moving pool some fifteen feet in length, which had a hospitable sand bar on our near side. I suggested that we wade out on the granite ledge, dive off this natural dam into the pool below, and with a few strokes, come to shore on the sand bar. Since it was my idea, the other two insisted that I should have the privilege of pioneering the route—so I ventured forth.

It was a simple matter to step from a boulder at river's edge, which stood a foot or so above the water level, across a space of eighteen inches to another boulder of similar size and height, then lower myself into the water at the edge of the dam. The flow here reached the calf of my leg, but became a few inches deeper as I moved carefully out along the granite edge toward midstream. After a few steps, the force of the moving water against my legs became much stronger than the weight of my body exerting its downward pressure, and I felt myself being swept off my feet. Deciding that I was not far enough out at this point for the water to be sufficiently deep to risk a dive, I slumped into a sitting position and slid over the polished granite of the dam into the pool a few feet below. From there I could either wade or swim out as the case may be. I never gave the situation another thought; I was getting a piece of the action, and it was fun.

It soon ceased to be fun, however; it is never fun when Death suddenly shows its face. After sliding over the dam and being submerged in the pool at its bottom, I attempted to square off and swim out, but, unaccountably, my arms and legs were propelled in all directions by a force beyond my control. Moreover, my body was being churned around so vigorously and erratically that I lost all sense of direction. I knew that I was in about five feet of water, because once in a while my foot would touch bottom at the same split-second that my head popped out of the pool. Such irony! Such frustration! Such a ridiculous situation! I, who could swim miles at a stretch, was drowning in water hardly neck high because I couldn't take the three or four strokes necessary to get out of this miserable whirlpool.

The volume and force of the water dropping into the pool below the dam had trapped me near its base, revolving my body heels over head without respite. This action was compounded by a powerful counter-clockwise whirl produced by a natural penstock at the side of the dam, a penstock formed by two boulders at the river's edge. Partially diverted by the dam, water raced through here to seek its level along the line of least resistance and then plunged down and immediately back toward the main body. Caught and held by both terrible forces working together, I was getting more action than I had bargained for.

Instinctively, I held my breath awaiting the few times my head was momentarily spewed out of the water, affording me a split-second gulp of air. Meanwhile the turning and churning went on and on. I wanted to yell to my companions on shore to pick up a broken tree limb lying on the ground nearby, extend it to me, and pull me in, but I did not have a chance to utter a sound, so fleeting was the fraction of a second my head was above water at any one time.

The situation became critical. The constant struggle, the occasional spasmodic gulp of air, and the interminable holding of breath was producing what I recognized as a state of euphoria. I had heard and read about this condition, which sometimes beckons a freezing person to a blissful death. Now it was happening to me in the river. Death was coming on, but oh-so-gently. My conscious mind told me not to fight it any longer—this was such an easy way to go. I thought of the wife and son that I had lost only six weeks before and wondered what I had to live for anyway. This seemed to be a good way out of my worldly troubles.

But my conscious mind did not take a very basic instinct into account: the will to survive. So, despite negative thoughts, I struggled on, and after what seemed an eternity, a glimmer of hope appeared. Howard and Jim, who, they told me later, had thought me to be putting them on, finally realized my predicament and did something about it. They took off their blue jeans, tied one leg of each together, and cast this lifeline across the surface of the water. As I came up for what surely would be one of the last few times, I caught a glimpse of them on the shore throwing out their improvised lifeline. The next time I was catapulted to the surface, I made a lunge for it and missed. The time after that I somehow got a hand on it but could not hold on. Finally, on the third try, I caught and held on desperately with my last remaining ounce of strength. They pulled me in, and I flopped at the river's edge and lay there like a hooked fish.

The death that I faced in the river that day was as near and real as it could be. I would most certainly have perished except for the emergency action of my two young friends. It must have taken me the best part of an hour to regain enough strength to trudge back up the hill to my cabin. There I dropped on my cot and didn't move a muscle for sixteen hours. Though young and strong, I was completely done in.*

Given a new lease on life, I began to throw off the melancholy that remained from the breakup of my marriage. I had long believed, with simple naïveté, that love conquers all, but at last I had to recognize that this was not always so. That recognition went a long way in making me a wiser and more mature person. Life gives, life takes away, and we carry on the best we can.

For four full months after my return to Sequoia as a permanent ranger, I regularly put in forty-four hours a week at the Ash Mountain checking station. My principal duty there was collecting entrance fees and dispensing information—pleasant enough, but hardly exciting. What really enlivened this assignment was the location of the checking station at the very hub of life at Ash Mountain.

In the 1930s and 1940s, this little stone cubicle, glass enclosed above waist-height on all sides, stood guard in the middle of the highway in the heart of the village, just one mile inside the park boundary. On one side, a path led a few feet up a gentle knoll to a rustic, two-story building constructed of cedar shakes. The chief ranger's office occupied the lower level, while the other park administrative offices spread over the larger upper floor. On the other side, a road descended into the maintenance area, the nucleus of operations. There was no visitor center at the time; the ranger on duty was the fount of all information for arriving tourists.

Thirty-two families lived in individual residences of from three to ten rooms each, spread out and well-hidden among the shrubbery and trees on both sides of the highway. There were six two-room bachelor cabins and a guest dormitory on

---

*Ironically, in a few short years Howard fell to a watery grave when he was lost in action over the Pacific as a fighter pilot during World War II; while Jim, in maturity, rose to a high position in the National Park Service as a regional director, and died of a heart attack shortly after retirement.

the side of the area that also contained shops, warehouses, and garages. These structures, perhaps eighty in all, were jumbled indiscriminately over some seventy-five acres and interlaced with a spider's web of hard-surfaced paths and roads.

Cloaked in an aura half twentieth-century and half Utopian, this mountain village of roughly one hundred inhabitants was unlike any community I have ever known. The checking station was its pulse. Not only must all traffic, local as well as tourist, stop here and make its business known, but the station also served as the clearing house for all the trivialities, petty bothers and errands, information of all kinds, and amenities of daily life.

The park ranger on duty at the checking station was the pivot of this life. We worked split shifts: one, from five o'clock A.M. to eight o'clock A.M. and noon to five o'clock P.M.; the other, from eight o'clock A.M. to noon and five o'clock P.M. to nine P.M. A night watchman was on duty from nine o'clock p.m. to five o'clock A.M., during which hours visitors could not enter the park. In spelling out this scene, I will take you through both shifts of a routine day in spring.

At five o'clock when I relieve the night watchman on duty at the station, the moon is sinking low in the western sky, casting a palely diffused glow over the world. Not a sound is to be heard except the steady and reassuring mumble of the river rushing along below the bluff. All things are asleep, and nothing mars the stillness of the night.

With the first faint hint of grayness in the east, here and there a bird breaks out with a few experimental chirps, much the same as members of a symphony orchestra tune for the concert. Soon warming to their song, these feathered musicians of the foothills get under way and sing the residents of Ash Mountain into wakefulness with a din that is excusable only because of its spontaneous joy in the welcoming of another glorious day. Night flees before the rapidly lightening eastern sky, and great blotches gradually turn into graceful oaks.

75

The first stir of human life abroad is the arrival of the high school bus at six forty-five. The driver is a sociable fellow with an honest and cheerful face, and he chats with me for a few moments, while the high school children gather for their twenty-one-mile ride. About the same time, the junior college bus pulls up to the station, headed now for school thirty-five miles away. The occupants of these buses have a sound and healthy look and their eyes are bright.

At full daylight, now about seven o'clock, we hoist Old Glory to the top to the flagpole, where it ripples reassuringly in the breeze.

Between seven-thirty and eight o'clock those employees who do not live at Ash Mountain trickle in from their homes down the canyon. They drive late-model automobiles.

About ten minutes to eight, people begin to stir around and wend their ways to work. They walk unhurriedly along paths that plunge through seas of waving green grasses and millions of wildflowers of multiple shapes and hues, past bush lupines resplendent in their royal purple dress, and alongside huge, red-limbed manzanitas, for it is only five minutes from the outermost dwelling to the offices and shops.

More often than not, there is time for a cheerful greeting and a neighborly reminiscence of the day or evening before, for there are no time clocks to punch. When they arrive at their jobs, the even flow of their lives continues. There are no nerves frayed by an early-morning crush of traffic, or lungs protesting against exhaust fumes. Seldom does anyone work under pressure, and then only during an emergency. They all wear informal and comfortable clothing, in the office and in the shop; their dress varies little from one season to the next, for they live at an elevation of 1,700 feet, above the dank winter fogs of the valley, in a climate as equable and pleasant as any on earth for nine months of the year.

At eight o'clock, dump trucks, stake-bodied trucks, and pickups begin rolling back and forth at their tasks. Uniformed rangers circulate on their assignments for the day. Up the highway from his home strides a tall, dignified figure of a man wearing a stiff-brimmed Stetson. He jauntily swings a cane and breathes in the fresh spring morning air with great gusto. Formerly a copper-haired soldier of fortune who made his mark as an adventurer, he turned to the comparative tranquility of superintending a national park. His hair now well-streaked with silver, he ably and forcefully runs his own little show, tempering the adventure and deviltry of his younger days with a gracious acceptance of a serene life in the place he loves best of all on earth.

Shortly after eight o'clock, the grammar school bus leaves with its load of bubbling and freshly scrubbed children. About this time the phone rings and I am informed that six inches of fresh snow have fallen last night in Giant Forest, a mere sixteen miles away; that tire chains are necessary to reach the Sequoia forest; and that skiing will be good until some time after noon. Although it is springtime and balmy here, it is winter within only a forty-minute drive, because each thousand-foot rise in elevation is equal to five hundred miles north latitude, and the climb is 4,700 feet.

By nine o'clock the milkman has come in and made his rounds. About eleven the mailman arrives with several pouches of mail. Before noon the groceryman has come in with his truck. I tell him to be sure to stop by the Browns' to pick up an order for tomorrow, because Mrs. Brown is giving a bridge luncheon the next day.

At a few minutes to noon, everyone drifts home for lunch. If their wives haven't beaten them to it, the men will go past the post office and pick up the mail. From noon to one, the place looks deserted. The silence is broken by a jangling phone. It's Mrs. Gregory, who says to be sure to tell the groceryman that he better make that pot roast six pounds because she is having the Davids over for dinner tomorrow night.

At one o'clock the men drift leisurely back to work. The main press of business is out of the way for the day, and frequently through the afternoon they gather in little knots of three or four to discuss world events and local topics of interest. They mull over matters of park policy by the hour, covering all aspects. After all, these things must be done right, and what better time and place to discuss them than now, sitting out in the balmy air and warm sunshine on a moss-covered boulder or on a nearby office porch during the lovely spring afternoon.

After two o'clock on any given afternoon, there is a flurry of traffic as the wives flock to their bridge parties. No more assiduous devotees of the game could be found.

In the meantime, I mustn't forget to have the laundryman stop at the Hamiltons and the Greens. And here is the money Mrs. Jackson left with me to pay the newspaperman. Also, the Graysons are going to San Francisco for a week to visit her parents, so please leave the evening paper at the Flacks until they get back.

Will I please give this pot of beans and this pie to the Marbles when they go through this evening on their way to the potluck supper at the Recreation Hall? Thanks so much.

About four, the grammar school bus brings back its precious load. The children jump and run, laugh and screech, as they tumble pell-mell from the vehicle. They dart here and there like a covey of quail that has just happened upon a lawn luscious with insects and worms.

Soon afterwards, the bridge party is over and the women reluctantly wander back home to prepare the evening meal. At five, the men crisscross each other's paths on the way home. What now for them? This is no haven of young men— the jobs these men hold are too sought-after to be attained in so short a time. These men are settled, secure, and satisfied, and average in the middle forties. Many have flower gardens to tend; some read the evening paper or listen to the radio; others drift several miles down the highway to some roadside inn and enjoy a beer or two; in season, a few dash down to the river and whip out a mess of delectable mountain trout.

At sunset I put Old Glory to bed. Around this time, about seven, Ash Mountain folk are enjoying their biggest meal of the day—soups, salads, meats, vegetables, fruits, and pastries. Nothing too fancy, just good, wholesome delicious food, well-cooked and enthusiastically received.

Afterward, some families settle comfortably with books,

radios, and lessons for a quiet evening at home. A few couples drive down the road for beers or cokes and idle chatter. Some will continue on into Visalia, a prosperous, beautiful little city of nine thousand people, thirty-four miles away, to see a movie or attend a concert or lecture. Once in a great while, some few become energetic enough to play a little tennis, take a stroll through the balmy evening, or, in season, swim in a delightful pool in the nearby river. But cozy, sociable dinner parties, with bridge afterward, are the most popular form of entertainment.

The scarlet sky of sunset fades into twilight and into an eerie dusk. Now a soothing and all-pervading darkness is upon me, stippled with a million little eternal lights. Soon again the world that we have watched today will be sunk in calm and restful sleep.

Besides the locals, I have seen and talked to many others—people who came from the forty-eight states as well as from other parts of the world. So skillfully blended into the landscape and hidden behind the huge old oaks are the indications of human habitation that very few tourists indeed realize that a community exists here. They would be even more surprised if they knew the community temperament.

For this is a temperament untainted by industrialism and commerce, enjoying all the advantages of twentieth-century science and culture, yet afflicted by none of its serious social problems. It is a temperament at once urban and rural. Here is security and peace to the highest degree attainable. Every man here knows that if this nation continues he will never be in want. By law, his job and his pension are for life. He, his wife, and his children need never go hungry, lack shelter, clothing, education, or the fundamental amenities of living as long as he does satisfactory work. Neither is there a taint of wealth to make him envious. Greed and exploitation and all the strife they cause in a nerve-racked competitive world are unknown here.

This is a temperament healthy and well-behaved. Absent are the causes of crime and misdemeanor. Houses and autos are rarely locked. Children are as safe as the deer, the fox, and the racoon that bound about the same ground. Theft, arson, rape, mayhem, or murder have never occurred. Flaring of tempers and bandying of barbed words are rare, and blows are never struck. Kindness and sociability are the norm.

On the other hand, lack of competition can act as an anaesthetic. Initiative can die a lingering but sure death. The creative instinct—painting, writing, music, sculpturing, etc.— is almost unknown. Life flows along the line of least resistance. Horizons become confined, almost to the walls of the canyon. Everything is done to maintain such pleasantries of life as exist, but nothing is done to stimulate and further the progress of man in his struggle toward sublimity. Some who live here may realize this, but perhaps they either lack the courage to go out and buck the competitive world with its accompanying strife, or they are content to live out a luxuriant vegetative life, along with the grasses, the shrubs, and the trees that flourish around them. Who is omniscient enough to say that they are right or wrong? In the end, it is for each of us to march to the beat of the drum we hear.

The pulse of the village has weakened, and the night holds sway. It is nine o'clock, so I turn the station over to the night watchman, my own work done.

The permanent ranger force was reinforced on May 1, the traditional date for temporary rangers to begin trickling in for the summer season. As a consequence, I was relieved from duty at the checking station for several weeks and assigned to other tasks. The nature of these for the first week of May can be no more succinctly described than by an examination of my diary. The verbatim notes read as follows:

WEDNESDAY, MAY 1

7:30 A.M.–3:30 P.M. Patrol Ash Mountain to West Boundary Cabin via North Fork, return via Ash Mountain Truck Trail.

6:00 P.M.–8:00 P.M. Patrol North Fork.

Approx. 100 fishermen
Average catch: 6 or 7
Fisherman checked: 31

Longest fish: 17″ (Chas. Hill)
Limits caught: 7
Mostly rainbow, a number of Lock Leven, and several
Dolly Varden, average size: 8″–9″

THURSDAY, MAY 2

Snow survey at Panther Meadow with George Brooks
Average depth: 80″
Water content: 40″

FRIDAY, MAY 3

Potwisha Fire-school along Ash Mountain truck trail.

SATURDAY, MAY 4

A.M.   Fire-school at Rec. Hall for E.C.W. Foremen, leaders,
etc.
P.M.   Inspect fire-fighting apparatus at Ash Mountain.

SUNDAY, MAY 5

Patrol Generals Highway Ash Mountain to Sherman Tree
with Jack Sinclair. Duty at Sherman Tree. Patrol G.F. to Lost
Grove and return to Ash Mountain.

MONDAY, MAY 6

A.M.   Burn brush at Potwisha with Ben Packard and George
Brooks.
P.M.   Off Duty.

TUESDAY, MAY 7

Off duty.

This break was only an aberration, however, because for
the following twelve months I stood regular duty at the checking
station. I did fill in once in a while at the chief ranger's office,
assisting the fire dispatcher and answering letters of inquiry,
and even more rarely made a patrol to Giant Forest and Lost
Grove. But those days were few and far between. Emergencies
to which I was dispatched were rare, but memorable.

One of the most challenging happened in midday during early summer. A report was received in the chief ranger's office that there was a fisherman in trouble in the canyon of the Marble Fork just below Deer Ridge, and I was sent to check it out. Jim Livingstone, superintendent of Potwisha CCC camp, met me at the Deer Ridge turnout on the Generals Highway with a coil of rope.

We had learned from his fishing companion that the man in trouble had a weak heart and just simply gave out when he tried to climb out of the chasm that dropped a thousand precipitous feet or so to the river. He wisely did not fight it and waited for help. That's where Jim and I came in.

We descended to the river without difficulty and found our man. Sure enough, he couldn't climb a step, but he was breathing easily and was apparently in no immediate danger. So Jim and I went about the business of hauling him out. We fashioned a loop in the rope, placing it around his body just below his armpits, and one of us got behind to steady him and push while the other climbed ahead pulling on the rope. We took it as easy as possible, but there is just no easy way for two people to hoist a good-sized man up such a steep slope. It was a herculean task performed under a blazing sun and through prickly brush that fought us almost every step of the way. Taking turns fore and aft of our helpless fisherman, we eventually got the job done.

But the worst was yet to come. The payoff for the good deed I had performed was a classic case of poison oak which had victimized me as, perspiring profusely, I unheedingly made my way up through the brush between the Marble Fork and the Generals Highway. It gave me fits for a week or so; the itching drove me crazy day and night. Calamine lotion didn't seem to help much as, painted white as a ghost, I suffered a penalty for helping to rescue a fellow man in distress. It was just another day in the life of a ranger.

Although I was kept on duty all summer at Ash Mountain, it passed in a pleasant, even enjoyable, manner. I developed new interests, met new friends, made occasional sorties to the dances in Giant Forest, and lolled at length with others

who found the swimming hole below the village to be a godsend of relief from the three-digit temperatures that characterized our summer days. I even dated a few girls, but was not
about to become involved with any of them. They were nice
company, but I could not have been more wary.

The winter that followed was a social stalemate. I went
out with a few girls, but couldn't get interested in any of
them. They just didn't have any attraction for me, as inevitably I compared them to the Florence of earlier days. Friends
were a solace, as was my closest companion and the joy of my
life, a handsome, sporty 1936 Chevrolet Coupe that I had
acquired early in the fall. Isolated as I was in the mountains,
this faithful vehicle gave me mobility and an outlet for my
questing spirit.

I was occasionally detailed to traffic control on weekends
at the Lodgepole and Wolverton winter sports areas on the
Giant Forest Plateau, but by far the most of my duty hours
were spent in the checking station at the entrance to the park.
It being the off-season, with little travel, I undertook the
study of Gregg shorthand to while away idle hours at the
station. It was an ideal situation to practice this skill, and I
became fairly proficient. I also did quite a bit of desultory
reading. After a few months of secretarial studies at night in
Visalia, I was offered a job not of my own seeking by one of
the Visalia banks that had heard about me through my
teacher. I declined it, although this would have brought me
into circulation in a town I rated the most attractive and
desirable in California. I was an outdoor man. The circum-
scribed life of an inside job with a financial institution just
didn't appeal to me, even though it offered the potential to
escape my loneliness.

In midwinter, at the age of thirty-one, I took up skiing, a
sport that had intrigued me for some time. At last the opportunity arose when it was decided that the park rangers in
Sequoia should become proficient on skis. Barry Caulfield, the
resident professional employed as a ski instructor by the con-
cessionaire in Giant Forest, volunteered to teach us the funda-
mentals. He agreed to give two lessons a week for about six

weeks. I put in many an hour alone on my days off, trudging up the steep slope at Wolverton under my own power and practicing my christies as I schussed down the hill at ever-increasing speeds. It was hard work, but stimulating and thrilling on the downhill run, and it laid the foundation for later grand adventures in the European Alps.

Occasionally I drove to Los Angeles to see my son, but things were not going well between his mother and me. It was a bad time. One evening she told me that she had begun divorce proceedings. The next morning was gloomy and there was a light rain falling. Driving around in a trance, I failed to avoid a collision at an intersection in Hollywood. The result was disastrous. Both vehicles were badly damaged and, although neither the other driver nor I was injured, a passenger in the other car wound up in the hospital for ten days. I had no insurance. That day was one of the worst I have ever known. Bedraggled, distraught, forlorn, and afoot, I wandered around Hollywood all day in a sort of daze, trying to get matters squared away so I could get back to Sequoia.

Fortunately I had friends who came to my rescue. One loaned me the money to have my car repaired. Another, a young attorney in Kingsburg, later appeared with me in Los Angeles at the hearing for an interlocutory decree of divorce and was able to bring about an out-of-court-settlement just before the case was called. This mandated reasonable child-support, but at my insistence alimony was permanently ruled out.

I returned to Sequoia breathing a little easier, but I still had a huge debt to liquidate, a debt which had been increased by an out-of-court settlement stemming from my negligence in the automobile accident. I believed I could do it in two years if I lived five or six months each in the backcountry. There, my government quarters (a two-room log cabin) would cost me five dollars a month, and by eating a spartan fare, I could manage my groceries on fifteen dollars a month. This would leave me, after a child support payment of thirty-five dollars, one hundred dollars a month to apply to my debts. Moreover, I felt that a carefree outdoor life in the high country, in an environment that I considered to be supremely spiritual and aesthetic, would rejuvenate my spirits and restore me to normal.

I knew that the ranger who had been in charge of the Kern Canyon-Mt. Whitney District was not returning, so a vacancy existed. Now, late in May, the snow was beginning to melt in the higher elevations, and it was about time to dispatch a ranger into the Kern to remain until the end of the hunting season in early October. I wanted that job, I needed that job, and I knew no one in the park was better qualified for that job.

In this extremity I turned to Chief Ranger Spigelmyre. I had not forgotten the time a few months before when my troubles were peaking (something not exactly a secret in our closely knit, small mountain community) and Spig had showed his true colors. One morning when no one was looking, this stocky, stubborn, blustering, bulbous-nosed old rapscallion of a Dutchman had slipped an arm around my waist and walked along this way with me a dozen steps and asked me to come to him whenever I thought he could help. This was the man who, perversely I had thought, relegated me to the backcountry in the summer of 1936 to deny me my heart's desire of returning to Giant Forest. Then, all that was at stake was a summer's amusement. Now all the chips were down. I would lay all my cards on the table and see if Spig was bluffing. I asked him to come down to my cabin where we could talk in private. There I told him, without mincing any words, where I wanted to spend the summer, where I *had* to spend the summer.

Spig was not bluffing. When the showdown came, I saw revealed a man of great kindliness and sympathy. His understanding heart was so large that it embarrassed him— yes, embarrassed him sometimes to such an extent that he had to flail his arms, shout till he was red in the face, and make life miserable in numerous little ways for those with whom he came in contact, all in order to hide his genuine humanity. Spig granted my request, and within a fortnight I was on my way to the Kern Canyon.

CHAGOOPA FALLS

6

Haven in the Kern

I knew something of what to expect on my new assignment. The district that I would be responsible for protecting covered a vast area: three hundred fifty-two square miles of the highest and most spectacular mountain terrain in the forty-eight states. I had studied its geography, geology, and history and listened to tales of its legendary beauty. Bounded on the east by Mt. Whitney and its sister peaks along the crest of the Sierra Nevada, on the north by the only slightly less towering ridges of the Kings-Kern Divide, and on the west by the imposing and snow-scarred heights of the Great Western Divide, forty peaks over 13,000 feet in elevation crowned these ramparts.

Among the finest features that had gained this area such renown was the Kern River Canyon. It is unique among the glacial-formed canyons of the Sierra Nevada, because it is the only one through which its stream does not flow in an easterly or westerly direction. The Kern River flows directly south from its headwaters, enclosed by many miles of high canyon walls, cleaving the Kern Canyon-Mt. Whitney District almost exactly in two.

Fading and undecipherable pictographs still to be found within a half-mile of the river testify that the first to see and know the Kern Canyon as we know it today were the people of some long-forgotten Indian tribe. Many, many years later, branches of the California valley tribes wandered in and used the canyon for hunting and fishing. Next came cowmen and sheepmen who ran their herds in the canyon and over the plateaus on both sides. Their stock beat well the faint trails of the Indians, and these herdsmen left a rich and picturesque heritage of names. Hunters and trappers came and found a paradise of game. In 1905 the area came under the control of the United States Forest Service. Eventually, improvements were made to encourage recreational travel. New trails were built, old ones were made better, and signs were placed. Telephone lines and pasture fences were erected. By 1926 so far-famed had the distinctive charm of this region become that it was placed under the protection of the National Park Service. This more than doubled the size of Sequoia National Park, which was established in 1890 with an area of two hundred fifty-two square miles. Now, in 1941, the baton had been passed to me personally. I would be able to see for myself this fabled land. The prospect could not have been more alluring or challenging.

On June 4, Johnny Wren, Frankie Dawson, and I rode out of the Ash Mountain Corrals with five saddle horses and eight mules. We were headed for the Kern Ranger Station eighty-five miles away, where I was to make my headquarters for the summer; Johnny and Frankie were to begin working the district trails. It was never feasible to take the stock directly into the Kern Canyon from Mineral King this early in the season, much less this year when snow levels in the area were the lowest since 1933. Both direct routes, one over Franklin Pass (11,400 feet) and the other over Farewell Gap (10,588 feet) and Coyote Pass (10,034 feet) were out of the question. Therefore, we had to make a circuitous route through the foothills before tackling the lower passes that permitted entry to the Kern Canyon from the south.

The first day we rode down to Three Rivers and followed the road up the South Fork of the Kaweah River to Kirk's place, where we camped for the night after covering sixteen miles.

The next day we left the beaten path to make our way through Grouse Valley and down the North Fork of the Tule River, through lovely rolling hills stippled with hardwoods fresh in bright spring dress and carpeted with a great profusion of wildflowers all colors of the rainbow. The Negus Ranch, twenty miles distant, was our destination, where we were favored with generous hospitality on our overnight stay.

On the third day, we left the Negus Ranch on a memorable ride up the Middle Fork of the Tule and the South Fork of the Middle Fork to Camp Nelson, where our ascent brought us into the pines. From there we switchbacked up the road to Quaking Aspen Meadow where we camped for the night after twenty-three miles in the saddle. That evening we were joined by Mr. J. A. Ramsay, a special agent for the Department of the Interior, who was to accompany us to the Kern Station to make an investigation concerned with the Conterno lease at Lewis Camp.

It is a twenty-six mile ride from Quaking Aspen Meadow to the Kern Station, a ride that demands strength and stamina from riders and stock alike to accomplish in one day. It is more often than not done this way to save a day's time and to eliminate the need for the extra unpacking and repacking required for a night's stopover at Trout Meadow. However, this being a first outing of the year, with tender spots here and there on our own persons, and heavy loads on the pack animals, together with newcomer Ramsay aboard, we decided to take the two-day option. So, after covering thirteen miles through Lloyd and Jerky meadows and across the Little Kern River, we stopped at Trout Meadow, always a delightful place to halt early in the year.

Kern Ranger District

1. FORESTER PASS
   13,160'
2. SHEPHERD PASS
   12,050'
3. MT. TYNDALL
   14,018'
4. MT. BERNARD
   13,990'
5. WALLACE LAKE
   11,450'
6. TULEINYO LAKE
   12,802'
7. MT. RUSSELL
   14,086'
8. MT. WHITNEY
   14,494'
9. TRAIL CREST
   13,480'
10. MT. MALLORY
    13,850'
11. MT. LECONTE
    13,960'
12. MT. LANGLEY
    14,027'
13. ARMY PASS
    11,475'
14. SIBERIAN PASS
15. BIG WHITNEY MEADOW
16. TUNNEL RANGER STATION
17. LITTLE WHITNEY MEADOW
18. LAKE SOUTH AMERICA
    11,941'
19. TYNDALL RANGER STATION
    10,333'
20. MOUNT WHITNEY R. S.
21. CRABTREE MEADOW
    10,337'
22. CRABTREE LAKES
23. MT. GUYOT
    12,300'
24. JUNCTION MEADOW
25. KERN HOT SPRINGS
26. CHAGOOPA FALLS

27. UPPER FUNSTON MEADOW
28. LOWER FUNSTON MEADOW
29. CONTERNO'S STORE
30. KERN DISTRICT R. S.
    6,458'
31. TOWER ROCK
    8,469'
32. KERN LAKES
33. COYOTE PASS
    10,180'
34. FRANKLIN PASS
    11,880'
35. FORESTER LAKE
    10,354'
36. LITTLE CLAIRE LAKE
    10,420'
37. SAWTOOTH PASS
    11,700'
38. BLACK ROCK PASS
    11,600'
39. LITTLE FIVE AKES
40. BIG FIVE LAKES
41. MORAINE LAKE
    9,302'
42. SKYPARLOR MEADOW
    9,440'
43. BIG ARROYO R. S.
44. MT. KAWEAH
    13,816'
45. RED KAWEAH
    13,754'
46. BLACK KAWEAH
    13,765'
47. KAWEAH GAP
    10,700'
48. NINE LAKE BASIN
49. TRIPLE DIVIDE PEAK
    12,634'
50. COLBY PASS
    12,080'
51. TABLE MOUNTAIN
    13,646'

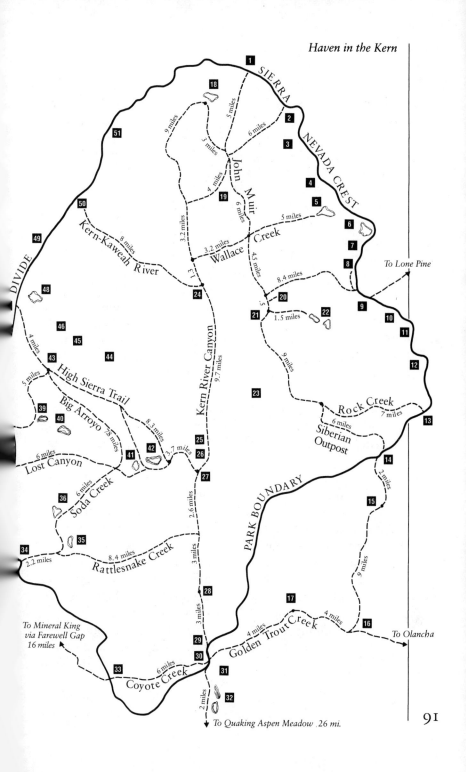

SIERRA

NEVADA CREST

To Lone Pine

DIVIDE

Kern-Kaweah River

John Muir

Wallace Creek

Kern River Canyon

High Sierra Trail

Big Arroyo

Lost Canyon

Soda Creek

Rattlesnake Creek

Rock Creek

Siberian Outpost

PARK BOUNDARY

Golden Trout Creek

Coyote Creek

To Olancha

To Mineral King
via Farewell Gap
16 miles

To Quaking Aspen Meadow , 26 mi.

9 miles

5 miles

6 miles

3 miles

4 miles

6 miles

5 miles

3.2 miles

3.2 miles

1.3

8 miles

45 miles

8.4 miles

1.5

1.5 miles

9 miles

9.7 miles

8.3 miles

.78 miles

3.7 miles

6 miles

6 miles

8.4 miles

2.2 miles

2.6 miles

3 miles

6 miles

4 miles

4 miles

2 miles

2 miles

9 miles

6 miles

7 miles

9I

The next day, June 6, we rode on through Willow Meadow to the Kern River and past the lakes to Lewis Camp on the southern boundary of Sequoia National Park, where Coyote Creek flows into the Kern River. After we unpacked, Johnny and Frankie put up the fence at the little meadow several hundred yards away that served as the pasture for park service stock, while Mr. Ramsay and I busied ourselves shaping up the kitchen and preparing the evening meal.

We had hardly settled into our sleeping bags for the night when Frankie was stricken about ten-thirty with an acute case of appendicitis. Here was my first emergency, and a critical one at that, before I had been more than seven or eight hours on the job in the Kern. I decided that if Frankie showed no improvement within the next hour, I would move him to Quaking Aspen Meadow at once. Meanwhile, Johnny gathered up two horses and a mule and saddled them, ready to ride. Eleven o'clock came and Frankie was still in considerable pain, so I asked Johnny to take him back to road's end at Quaking Aspen.

Laying this on Johnny was an extremely difficult decision for me to make. As the official protector of life and limb in my district, as well as being the younger and perhaps the stronger of the two of us, I felt an overwhelming need to take Frankie in myself; he was my direct responsibility. But when I weighed the fact that most of the ride would be made on a dark, moonless night, that I had been over the trail only once, and that Johnny had ridden it numerous times over the years and knew it well enough to ride it blindfolded, I had to let common sense prevail. To ask a man in his mid-sixties—twice my age—to ride a total of forty miles in less than twenty-four hours, with a hard day's work sandwiched in between, was not at all to my liking, but Frankie's life was at stake.

After Johnny and Frankie departed about midnight, I tried to contact Chief Ranger Spigelmyre. The station radio was inoperative, and the direct telephone line from the Kern to Ash Mountain was severed and down in other places due to the storms of the past winter. Finally, about one thirty A.M., I was able to reach Spig through the U.S. Forest Service line running south. As a consequence, when Johnny and Frankie reached Quaking Aspen about seven o'clock A.M., there was a park service vehicle and driver waiting to take Frankie immediately to the Woodlake Hospital. There he underwent surgery later in the day, and survived. Johnny Wren, of course, was the man who made this possible. It was little wonder that I grew to love this fine, good-natured man and to enjoy his companionship and reliability over subsequent years.

During my first five days at the ranger station, I put the short-wave radio into operation, worked successfully on the water line that led into the kitchen from Coyote Creek, set up the outdoor shower, cleaned out the cabin, tidied the front and back yards, repaired the pasture fence and nearby drift fence, cleaned up the tool and paint shelter, and repaired the barley box. I also buried what remained (head and hide) of a large American black bear that had apparently died during hibernation in an old trapper's shanty on the northern edge of the ranger pasture.

Then Johnny Wren and I rode into Quaking Aspen for supplies and to bring back Leonard Shellenbarger (who was to be my assistant at Mt. Whitney Ranger Station) and his wife, as well as a trail-crew replacement for Frankie Dawson. Following that came a week of moving the outside toilet, rebuilding the food cooler, and maintaining the telephone line from the station to the top of Coyote Pass.

On July 10, I helped Temporary Ranger Shellenbarger and his wife move to their summer home at the Mt. Whitney Ranger Station and put up the nearby corral fence. The next day we sawed firewood and put up the tourist pasture fence at sprawling Crabtree Meadow.

By the time I got back to the Kern Ranger Station two days later, Bill and Lucia Neelands had arrived and set up the summer camp that they had enjoyed for years, midway between the ranger station and Conterno's place. They became my fast friends for their remaining years. Mrs. Neelands came by her love for the Kern Canyon naturally, for she was the niece of Nathaniel Langford of the Washburn-Langford-Doane expedition whose exploration of the Yellowstone region in 1870 led to the establishment of the national park system.

Conterno's Camp and Store was a small operation run by Jules and Mae Conterno that, in addition to stocking a limited number of foodstuffs, provided meals and tent shelters for passersby in need. It was located just across the trail from the meadow that served as the pasture for NPS stock. The Conternos were a fixture here even before this area became a part of Sequoia National Park in 1926. Their site was called Lewis Camp; how it derived its name I do not know. After the park service took over this area, a ranger cabin was built on the trail about three hundred yards south of the Conterno place, on the north bank of Coyote Creek. Since then, the name Lewis Camp is often used to designate the Kern Ranger Station due to its proximity to this historic connection.

The Conternos were good neighbors. However, they rarely came up the trail to the ranger station because they were fully occupied with taking care of their camp and store—a "mom and pop" business in a corner of the wilderness. Since I always had to pass their place to wrangle my stock and again on most of my patrols, I saw them often and frequently stopped to chat with them for a few moments. On evenings when I was free and wanted to learn how the war was progressing on the Eastern Front, I would walk down to their camp and join them and the Neelands in a circle around their radio for an hour or two. There we sat, healthy, comfortable, and well-fed, with not a worry in the world, deep in the embrace of a balmy star-lit summer night, our world limited to the walls of the canyon on either side, while the Russians and the Germans were hell-bent on destroying one another in some mad, faraway world.

Jules Conterno was a sturdy, taciturn, self-effacing man in his sixties, very much representative of the honest and industrious rural French stock from which he had descended. I liked Jules. He never spoke a word in anger, and he was ever-ready to lend a helping hand, whatever the occasion. I soon learned that I could depend on him.

Mae Conterno was something else. You could usually find her sitting in a canvas lounge chair, out in the pleasant sunshine in front of her tidy little camp. Never at a loss for words, she took up with where she had left off with the person before. Her brooding blue eyes deepened with interest at your approach, but it was not the eyes that captured your attention. It was that amazing, incredible complexion. Many a sweet sixteen would have envied the healthy glow and satiny texture of the skin, and the rose-petal cheeks so resplendently abloom on the face of this matriarch of sixty. Framing her cherubic countenance was a mass of washed-out black hair, deeply shot with silver, brushed back all the way around the front, wiry ends straggling in a fuzzy halo, its mass caught in a roll at the back.

What long ago must have been an attractive figure had been padded by the years until its feminine contours were more than ample and somewhat infirmly anchored. Mae invariably was bareheaded. Her serviceable, plain blue men's workshirt seemed always freshly laundered and carefully pressed. Blue denim trousers and some old, scuffed, low-heeled, brown oxfords further ensured the comfort of this wilderness woman.

The Conternos kept a register of all who passed by their place. Rare indeed was the traveller who could escape Mae's vigilance ensuring that each inscribe his or her name, address, and destination. On the few occasions when she met resistance, Mae persuaded the visitor that this information would be of great assistance to the ranger in case of an emergency. And she was right.

Thus, for more than a score of years, Mae kept tab on the thousands of hikers and horseback riders, tourists and rangers, dudes and hillbillies who streamed back and forth along the trail in front of her camp. She forgot very few of them, and she remembered much of the account they had made of themselves while in her presence. She was at once the historian and the journalist, the prophet and the gossip, of this small world. Openly entertaining, hospitable, and pleasant, she could become, as soon as her visitor rounded the next turn in the trail, gossipy and sometimes sharp-tongued.

So, while I sat and chatted and sometimes ate at her table some of the best cooked food in the mountains, I hugely enjoyed listening to her satire on others. But I knew that the next day, while I was miles away on patrol, if something came up that demanded my attention, she would say, "Where is that no-good ranger? Never is around when he is needed. It's a pity they send men like that out here. I'm going to call headquarters and report him. The worst man we've ever had on this job." Nevertheless, when her comments were eventually reported to me, I chuckled to myself, called her a gossiping old battleaxe, and went back for more.

On July 15, Colonel John R. White returned to Sequoia to take over as superintendent, the position he had relinquished on January 1, 1939, when he left to serve in the Washington office of the National Park Service and after that, as regional director of the Southwest and Western regions. The story of Colonel White and his influence and guidance in making Sequoia National Park the great American natural resource that it is has been told over and over again; he is legendary. Suffice it to say that he immediately showed where his heart lay by striking out on horseback for the Kern District within two weeks of his return.

I met Colonel White and his party at Kaweah Gap, the western boundary of my district, on the 29th of July. We then rode together on across the Chagoopa Plateau and dropped down into the Kern Canyon to camp overnight at Upper Funston Meadow. This was a popular place to camp because of its location and abundant forage for stock, but the mosquitoes were bad. To illustrate just how large and ferocious they were, let me tell you in his own words what Colonel White related to us at breakfast next morning: "I was awakened during the night by an unusually heavy weight that settled on my sleeping bag. When I rose up a bit to see what was going on, I saw two huge mosquitoes, and they were arguing about what to do with me. I heard one ask the other, 'shall we eat this SOB right here or carry him home with us?'" The colonel did not say what happened then, but he made his point.

We saddled up after breakfast, and I rode with the colonel and his party up the canyon to Chagoopa Falls, where he inspected the campgrounds. Earlier in the summer, while shaping up this site, I had knocked down and removed a small lean-to that in my view was nothing more than an unsightly boar's nest that was cluttering up the landscape. The colonel asked me about this, and when I told him, he seemed a bit upset that, as he put it, the campground had lost this bit of "color." However, he let it pass and said no more about it. He knew from my Redwood Meadow days of my predilection for making things spic and span in my backcountry jurisdiction, an effort he himself had commended me for personally more than once.

The colonel and his party rode on to Junction Meadow and up to Mt. Whitney Ranger Station while I returned to the Kern Ranger Station. Three days later I rode up to Little Whitney Meadow on Golden Trout Creek to escort the colonel's party down to the Kern Ranger Station. They had come from Mt. Whitney Ranger Station over Guyot Pass into Rock Creek and thence over Siberian Pass to Big Whitney Meadow before reaching Little Whitney. Since they spent the next day at the station, I had a good chance to have a long personal talk with the colonel about how to speed up advancement in the National Park Service. He unequivocally recommended that, as soon as I could, I arrange a spot for myself in the Washington office. Given my career aspirations at the time, it was good advice, but I was loath to even think about leaving the Kern for the time being.

Julius Asa (Ace) Peck was the district ranger responsible for overseeing activities in all of Sequoia's backcountry. He was stationed at Atwell Mill Ranger Station, the hub of nearby activities, and he had his hands full. As a result, I saw him only once during the summer, in mid-July when he and I made an overnight patrol up the canyon to Chagoopa Falls so

97

that he could inspect the condition of the canyon trail. There was a bad spot a mile or so north of the Kern Ranger Station that flooded during the June runoff every year; eventually the floodwaters subsided and a bog remained. The trail needed to be realigned here, so we selected a new route.

If anyone had suggested to Ace Peck that he was a prototype of the old-time ranger, he would have scoffed—understandably so, because Ace Peck was a unique individual. Be that as it may, the fact was that Ace embodied all those attributes that made the old-time rangers the men that they were: self-reliant, resourceful, steadfast, courageous, pragmatic, mentally and physically tough.

Ace was a great guy to work for; he possessed tact and subtlety that would be a credit to a polished diplomat. He never gave orders or instructions; rather, he simply went over the problem with me and once in a while slipped in a suggestion. He gave a man credit for being an intelligent and conscientious subordinate who didn't need a picture drawn to follow through. It worked.

Ace was a soft-spoken man with a superb dry humor. When the occasion called for it, he would use this humor to camouflage the barbs he directed at fools, whom he did not suffer gladly. Indications of his disdain were classic: a startling change etched in the lines of his face, the look in his eye, a snort of disgust. Ace was characteristically easy-going, but he was not a man to cross. Behind that calm exterior lay strands of steel that were forbidding indeed; I never saw Ace angry, but I was told that with enough provocation, he could really rage.

Among other reasons, I was drawn to Ace by his unfailing wit and his repertoire of tales, some tall and some authentic, which made him great company. He was easy to get along with, and I always felt at ease in his presence. His native intelligence and wit were credits to, and enriched, his way of life. Best of all, Ace Peck was a loyal and steadfast friend whom it was my good fortune to know and occasionally visit for forty years until he died in his Three Rivers home in 1981 at age ninety-two.

My life as a backcountry ranger in the High Sierra was varied, challenging, and exciting. I spent half of my time on patrols throughout the district and the remainder on duty at the Kern Canyon Ranger Station. The patrols led me along white-water rivers and placid streams, beside sparkling lakes, across lush meadows, through park-like forests, into alpine regions carpeted with delicate flowers, over high mountain passes, and even to the summit of Mt. Whitney, at 14,494 feet, the highest point in the forty-eight states. I also sought out and explored half-obliterated trails, familiarizing myself with every possible line of communication, pioneering a good part of the way. My diary reveals that in five months in 1941, I covered a total of 1,344 miles of this sublime terrain on horseback.

I was generally able to balance my days on patrol against periods at the cabin station. When the attraction of one function began to wear thin, I would shift gears and get into the other mode—a perfect arrangement. Until October, there was not a single day at the station that I was without either official or personal guests; I convoyed them in and out of the district, first from Quaking Aspen and later over Franklin Pass or Farewell Gap from Mineral King, coordinating their arrivals and departures with official need for supplies. Sometimes my guests rode with me on my patrols. Despite their presence, I carried on my station chores: cutting firewood, keeping the water supply in operation, repairing the cabin and its facilities, shoeing horses and mules, doing laundry, writing reports, keeping tabs on passersby and furnishing them information, maintaining the cabin and premises in a clean and orderly condition, and repairing equipment.

If you would like to get acquainted with the Kern Canyon, join me on an overnight patrol from the Kern Ranger Station to Junction Meadow and return.

Today, this eighteen-mile stretch is a veritable Garden of Eden that enhances the renown of this stupendous cleft in the earth. But it wasn't always this way. Long ago great glaciers thrust their icy fingers over the newly formed Sierra Nevada of California. They ground and gouged their way over and through this mass of solid granite, eventually melting away and leaving exposed gigantic U-shaped furrows, lifeless and ugly, the sister glacial canyons of the Sierra. Life and beauty filtered in with the passing of centuries, and the region's canyons became as they are today. One of these is reputed to be just a little more beautiful, just a little more spectacular, just a little more enchanting than all the rest. This is the canyon of the Kern River.

Let us make our patrol sometime in July. This will allow us to miss the heavy trail traffic which occurs in August. We will not bother to take a tent. (I never packed one in the six full summers I spent in the backcountry of Sequoia National Park, and I never got wet, day or night.) As a precaution, though, we can tie slickers to the back of our riding saddles; unless we are caught in a hailstorm or meet a light sprinkle of rain, there will be no use for them. Don't worry about the weather, it will be absolutely ideal day and night, as it is from June through August. On the average, skies are clear twenty-one days a month; partly cloudy seven, and cloudy only two. Precipitation, when it does fall (on an average of twice a month), is generally light. In September, the days cool off a bit, and the nights become frosty.

Now that I have briefed you on what to expect, let's mount our horses and see what we can see. As we ride out of the Kern Ranger Station, we note that the trail leads south across Coyote Creek, perhaps a hundred feet or so away. If we were to proceed in that direction, we would come to the park boundary in a few yards and pass Kern Lakes in a mile or two, ultimately reaching a number of southerly points below the park. We could also cross Coyote Creek, turn right, and immediately begin the steep ascent over Coyote Pass and drop into the Little Kern watershed before climbing over Farewell Gap to Mineral King. But our direction on this trip is to the north.

As we start out through the pines and incense cedar that tower in open-park fashion over the ranger station and environs, you hear the rumble and roar of the Kern River, unseen, but only a hundred yards away. If you are alert, you may catch a glimpse of the twin fawns, the litter of Columbia grey squirrels, or a covey of grouse that frequent the area. You cannot miss Tower Rock, thrusting its bulky, precipitous mass of granite high into the sky above us just across the river.

In about two hundred yards, we come to the trail that leads to the river, across the suspension bridge, and abruptly up the Golden Trout Creek drainage to Tunnel Meadow and other points on the Kern Plateau before descending into Owens Valley or climbing over Siberian Pass and dipping down into Rock Creek.

Another hundred yards takes us past Conterno's Camp and Store and the ranger pasture opposite. After letting ourselves through the drift fence a short distance away, our path winds near the river and alongside the talus that has broken and dropped from the cliffs on the left. From now on, all the way to Junction Meadow, we will travel up a canyon that lies almost as straight as an arrow, averages a quarter-mile in width, and presents walls on either side that rise precipitously two thousand feet and more above the canyon floor. In the bottom of the canyon, the trail leads through thickets of fir and cedar, clumps of quaking aspen and poplar, and park-like acres of pine and grass. Through it all, depending on its mood, the Kern River purls and ripples, glides and coasts, boils and rages, changes from a murmuring child to a howling demon and back again.

Three miles from the Kern Ranger Station we pull alongside Lower Funston, a large expanse of green and inviting meadow. We find campers here, for most of whom the main purpose in life is fishing; here they do well indeed. Their prey is the famous Kern River Rainbow, a mountain trout full of fight and flavor and as beautiful a trout as swims. Bait is seldom used here, except by the novice. The favorite and most efficient flies are the Royal Coachman, Black Gnat, and Grey Hackle. If you try your luck here, chances are that you will catch your limit of fifteen fish, or seven pounds and one fish, in good time; or you may prefer to try the waters at Junction

KERN CANYON AND THE KAWEAHS FROM TOWER ROCK

THE OLD SWINGING BRIDGE ACROSS THE
KERN RIVER NEAR LEWIS CAMP

THE KERN RANGER STATION

THE KING OF THE KERN SURVEYS HIS DOMAIN
(THE KAWEAHS FROM SKYPARLOR MEADOW)

Meadow when we make camp. In either case, hooking a twelve-inch Rainbow is almost guaranteed, and whatever you take will taste delicious right out of the stream into the frying pan. Before we leave Lower Funston, you may see the golden eagle I saw here earlier this month.

Three miles farther north we cross Rattlesnake Creek where, earlier this year, I was turned back by a torrent I judged to be too dangerous to ford. Now it still flows wide, but the water level is safely low, just a stone's throw from its confluence with the Kern. A short distance beyond the ford, the trail turns abruptly left (west), switchbacking up the Rattlesnake Gorge, eventually crossing Franklin Pass and dipping into Mineral King. The creek and gorge are appropriately named, because rattlesnakes abound in the area. In fact, the chances are better than even that we will see one or more sometime today, because this dangerous reptile favors the canyon as much as we do.

Three more miles bring us to Upper Funston Meadow, a rival of Lower Funston as a camping and fishing favorite. This is where my friend, Jay N. Holliday, caught a twenty-inch Rainbow in mid-July. It is also a popular stopover for horseback parties, as there is good pasturage for stock at the junction with the High Sierra Trail. This trail reaches the canyon from the west, after having wound its way from Crescent Meadow in Giant Forest, past Bearpaw Camp and Hamilton Lake, over Kaweah Gap, and across the Chagoopa Plateau, skirting the magnificent Red and Black Kaweahs and Mt. Kaweah before dropping precipitously into the Kern.

Just above Upper Funston we cross a bridge over the Kern and proceed up the eastern side of the river. Almost at once, on our left, Chagoopa Creek leaps off the Chagoopa Plateau into the Kern in an impressive fall of sixteen hundred feet. Still farther on, perhaps a mile or so north of Upper Funston, we come to a place you will certainly want to visit: the Kern Hot Springs. No doubt you will want to rid yourself of accumulated trail dust and relax in the natural hot water that is piped into the concrete tub. We may have a long wait outside the bathhouse, because there is no more popular a place in the

Kern Canyon than the Hot Springs. I have known as many as seven persons at one time waiting their turn in the tub; any evening in July and August finds the place crowded. In case you want to cool off afterwards, I guarantee you can do this effectively by submerging yourself in the icy waters of the river, only a few steps behind the bathhouse.

By the time we reach Junction Meadow, we may have seen as many as thirty or thirty-five deer browsing in the meadows, loping through thickets of fir and cedar, or timidly questioning the right-of-way of the trail. Perhaps five or six times a vision a silvery grey has flashed across our path as a large Columbia grey squirrel, the most beautiful of all canyon inhabitants, leaps from tree to tree. It would not be uncommon to see an American black bear now scampering, now crashing its marauding way through the canyon bottom. We may have even seen a porcupine waddling between the pines. Coyotes are present but seldom seen. Multitudes of birds flash in the sunlight and sing their hearts out in the cottonwoods and poplars. Junction Meadow itself is an especially favorable location for wildlife.

I regret that I can't spend any more time on this patrol, because I'd like to take you up into the High Sierra over one or more of the trails that diverge from Junction Meadow and ascend to the higher elevations. If we turn west, we would climb up into the marvelous, little-frequented Kern-Kaweah Basin that leads to Colby Pass. If we continue straight ahead, we would climb up to Lake South America and through its beautiful alpine gardens, linking up with the John Muir Trail below Forester Pass on the Kings-Kern Divide. If we turn east, we would follow the High Sierra Trail up Wallace Creek to the John Muir Trail and on to Crabtree Meadow and the Mt. Whitney Ranger Station, finally emerging on the summit of Mt. Whitney.

But enough of day-dreaming. Let's unpack, turn our stock loose (they won't go far, because there is a drift fence down the trail), spread our sleeping bags, build a fire, and put those freshly caught fish in the frying pan. As patrols go, it has been a very easy day, but if you are a tenderfoot, it will have been long enough. You will be ready to turn in shortly after night falls.

The next day we will return to the Kern Ranger Station, but in doing this we will not recross the trail bridge at Chagoopa. Instead, we will pick our way down the east side of the river in what will be rough going a lot of the time. You will get a taste of pioneering through a tangled wilderness until we reach a point opposite Rattlesnake. There we find a trail that gradually improves from fair to good by the time we reach the ford over the Kern River just above the Golden Trout Creek confluence. If you rode this last six-mile stretch with me a few months from now, you would see an autumn wonderland that affords the best color in the canyon. It amounts to a private park inasmuch as I never saw another human being there.

And that two-day patrol, my friends, is a sample of what life can be in the Kern Canyon. But do not come and roam here unless you are willing to be enslaved by its charms. Its beauty and peace and harmony will entrance you. Once it has you in its power, it will never release you the rest of your days.

It was smooth sailing up and down the canyon trail between the Kern Ranger Station and Junction Meadow. Probably nowhere in the district was the going better. In stark contrast was the trail that climbed from Mineral King over Sawtooth Pass and dropped down past Columbine Lake to the head of Lost Creek. In view of a proposed outing by the Sierra Club in 1942 over this trail, I rode out of Mineral King in early September to ascertain its condition.

I found it passable for saddle stock on the Mineral King (USFS) side, but highly inadvisable to use, about the worst bit of trail I encountered where travel by stock was a concern. Near the top of Sawtooth Pass, I tied up my horse and dropped down afoot into the park side. My report to the chief ranger, dated September 26, 1941, contains the following account, which I cite as an example of a backcountry ranger's responsibility to protect the travelling public in his district.

The trail is impassable in at least four places on the park's side between the pass and Columbine Lake, due to "jump-offs" from six to ten feet in height. In addition there is a great deal of slick rock to traverse, which is dangerous at the best. This trail can be fixed up on the park side without too great an expense, as the grade is good and the greater part of the section is in fair shape. However, one thing to consider here is that even had the trail itself been in good shape, it would be impassable in two places, due to snowdrifts, one extending four- or five-feet deep clear across the pass itself, and one six- or eight-feet deep in a narrow gully on the park side, with water running underneath and no way around. This was on September fifth. In view of the short season it could ordinarily be used, and the condition of the trail on the Mineral King side, it is highly questionable whether it should be touched. Until, and if, something is done, I strongly recommend that a large sign be placed at the top of Sawtooth Pass, blocking the trail and advising that the trail beyond there is impassable to stock and has been abandoned. This sign should be made this winter and erected next spring.

I climbed back over the pass and, since it was still early in the afternoon, decided to continue on foot to the top of Sawtooth Peak. It is appropriately named: on a clear day its jagged, sawtooth shape is prominent on the skyline even from the San Joaquin Valley to the west. From the top of Moro Rock, it is much more sharply and impressively outlined. At any rate, whenever it had come into my vision, whether from near or afar, it presented a challenge that someday I intended to meet. I'd never have a better chance than this day, so up I went.

It was an easy ascent up an open, moderately inclined slope of decomposed granite that comprised its western bulwark. The view, as is the case from the top of most peaks in the Sierra, was spectacular, but this one afforded the extra attraction of lovely, sparking Columbine Lake at its base. Alone on this high mountain top, I removed my clothing and took a sunbath for about thirty minutes. I lay on the topmost ledge in my private solarium in the Sierra, only a few feet from where it dropped from its overhang hundreds of feet. In time, I returned to my saddle horse and led him down the rough trail almost to Mineral King before I mounted. Such was the life of a backcountry park ranger in Sequoia—or at least what one ranger made of it.

During the last ten days of my sojourn in the Kern that year I saw no one. It was a rather welcome respite, riding the park boundary on the outlook for deer hunters in the glowing colors of autumn during the day, and getting in lots of good reading at night. When at last a heavy snow set in and it was obviously time to get out, I was ready to leave my kingdom; all that I had expected from it had materialized—and more. I had been occupied with one thing and another to such an extent that I did not have time to think of my troubles; they had receded to some vague and distant corner of my mind.

So it was that, late in October, I closed the station and, in snow up to eighteen inches deep, crossed over Farewell Gap and dropped into Mineral King. I then went down the road to the Atwell Mill Ranger Station to conclude a twenty-eight mile ride. There I quartered and fed my stock and stayed the night. My hosts were District Ranger Ace Peck and his wife Esther. It was a joyous and memorable occasion, my first contact with human society in some time, with a couple whose company was invariably cheerful and heart-warming. Next day, I rode the twenty-two miles on down the long, sinuous automobile road that follows the East Fork of the Kaweah River and so to the Ash Mountain Corrals with my horses and mules, closing out my backcountry life for the year. I was content, comfortable that I was leaving my domain in the protective embrace of winter until I could return in the spring.

The ensuing seven months were hardly more than a marking of time. My primary duty assignment in that interval consisted of working a split shift at the entrance checking station, broken occasionally by road patrols, weekends on duty at the winter sports areas, and, in the spring, fishing surveillance.

Less than a month after I came in from the Kern, I lost a friend when Judge Walter Fry died on November 18 at the age of eighty-two. I was not alone in this loss. Everyone who loved the Big Trees and all the elements of nature that mark this region as something extra-special also suffered, because directly or indirectly, he enriched their lives by the way he led his own. A modest, kindly, gracious, even-tempered man, completely devoted to the best interests of the park and an authority on its flora and fauna, he served nobly for thirty-six years as park ranger, chief ranger, superintendent, and U. S. Commissioner. As Colonel John R. White, his successor as superintendent, stated in his first monthly report: "It would be almost impossible to overstate the affection and esteem in which Judge Fry is held by both park employees and visitors." How true! The judge often stopped by the checking station to chat with me while I was on duty there. I was flattered, because I knew I was in the presence of a legend. It was a sad day when we said goodby to Walter Fry, but one thing about that occasion that I remember with pride is the honor that befell me to serve as one of his pallbearers.

After the services in Visalia were concluded, I returned to my bachelor quarters at Ash Mountain. My one room was small and inconvenient, but adequate: in one of a group of six similar two-room cabins, with a shared kitchen next door and a common washroom across the street sixty feet away. This setup was awkward at best, but in bad weather it forced us into a series of spirited sprints between shelters. I could not complain, however, about this Spartan accommodation, because my five-dollar monthly rent was a factor in helping me reduce the size of my financial problems. Furthermore, I did not spend much of my time there except to eat and sleep.

Since there were no single women anywhere near my age residing in Ash Mountain, I was compelled to go far afield for feminine society. I rode forth, not as the loner of an age long past who sallied forth on his faithful steed, but behind the wheel of my faithful Chevrolet. The range of my social activity that winter extended from Fresno to Los Angeles, with intermediate sorties into Exeter, Woodlake, Visalia, and Lindsay. I frequented the public library and the movie theater in Visalia, where I also did my shopping and attended lectures at the high school when national celebrities came to speak.

Sometime early that winter, I took another tack in an effort to escape my loneliness, when I sought the society of my contemporaries in church. I had been born, baptized, and bred in the Christian Church, so naturally my first thought was of the Christian Endeavor meetings held on Sunday evenings. Thus it was that one Sunday evening I left Ash Mountain headed for the Christian Church in Visalia. I never got there.

Total darkness had set in by the time I reached the little community of Three Rivers, and a light rain was falling. A mile or two down the road, still in the foothills, I dimmed my lights for a car approaching from the opposite direction. The roadway was clear as it drew near, but the glare of its headlights momentarily blinded me as we passed. At the split-second that my sight came back into focus there appeared in my lane of the roadway, so close that I barely caught a glimpse of it over the hood of my vehicle, what I thought was a bundle of clothing. Immediately there were two minor bumps as the front and rear wheels passed over the object.

I stopped to investigate and discovered that I had run over a man. An habitual drunkard, he had gone to the market in Three Rivers that night to buy some meat, had stopped at a bar and drunk far too much, and had been seen staggering home down the road. The conclusion was inescapable that he had passed out and fallen in the road shortly before I came along.

Sure, I felt sorry for this man and his wife and his two little boys, six and eight; I hoped mightily that he would survive, but he was dead on arrival at the hospital. I also felt sorry for myself. I rightly felt no guilt, but the shock I experienced was horrendous. I could not help but wonder, "what next?" When was Fate ever going to stop beating up on me?

The irony inherent in this incident is sharp. For the first time in many years I had been moved to attend church services. Because I followed through on this impulse, a man died—both of us victims of unpredictable forces that subvert our best intentions. I did not try again.

At this same time other forces were at work which were to have a profound effect on my life—in fact, within a year, to turn it around. Germany had invaded Poland just three days after the birth of my son, and all of Europe was engulfed in the flames of a great war. I was an interested but aloof observer. I had my own personal battles to fight, and my concentration was on surviving them. Then came Pearl Harbor, a few days after the highway fatality. I was on duty at the Ash Mountain checking station when, about twelve-thirty Sunday, December 7, 1941, a tourist leaving the park stopped momentarily to tell me that he had just heard over the radio about the Japanese attack. Now it had become a different ballgame—one in our own backyard. I was caught up in the patriotic fervor that swept the nation and wondered what my contribution might best be.

It was also at this time that I met, through a mutual friend, a young lady who, through all of 1942, was to become the most important player on the stage of my life. Alice was somebody special. Vivacious and intelligent, she had a sharp mind and a dedicated competence that served her well as the personal secretary to the president of a large company whose name was known in virtually every household in southern California. Pretty and pert and mercurial, her volatility was stimulating. She was a divorceé with a son only a few years older than my own. Aside from that, we had much more in common. We found in each other a companionship and an affection—albeit somewhat tempestuous at times—that was good for both of us. Though she lived and worked in Los Angeles, we never passed up an opportunity to be together.

After exploring my options at length in early 1942, I decided to apply for a direct commission in the Armed Forces of the United States. I appeared to qualify on two counts, so I submitted the required paper work in applications for (1) a first lieutenancy in the Army Air Force's counter-sabotage effort, and (2) a junior grade lieutenancy in the U. S. Navy, in command of a gun crew guarding liberty ships transporting munitions and supplies across the North Atlantic Ocean.

Meanwhile, weeks passed pleasantly on the job and on frequent trips to Los Angeles to visit my son and Alice. I resumed my skiing at the Wolverton slope every time I had a chance. Twice, in company with a fellow ranger, I made cross-country snow-gauging sorties to Panther Gap to measure the depth and water content of the snow pack—one on snow-shoes and one on skis. Given this wintry mountain milieu and it challenges, both were exciting adventures.

My duties also took me frequently to Lodgepole that winter. A large area at one edge of the campgrounds had been leveled and intermittently flooded with hot water that froze into a smooth surface fit for ice-skating. This rink proved very popular with the residents of nearby communities in the San Joaquin Valley; they converged there on weekends in such numbers that we had to control the movement of their vehicles in and out of the limited parking space. Generally there were two of us working together on this. I had never ice-skated, so every once in a while when things were slack, I would slip in an hour or so on the silver blades. I learned fast and came to enjoy the sport; by winter's end I had become fairly proficient.

Winter turned to spring, which brought its normal transfusion of fresh and colorful beauty to the foothills, closely followed by the advent of fishing season. This meant that it was time to prepare for my return to the Kern Ranger Station, so I began to get my stock and equipment together.

7

With a Song in My Heart

I had not received any response to my applications for a commission by the time it was necessary to return to my station in the Kern Canyon for the 1942 season. Hence, again with Johnny Wren and another trail crew member, George Lacy, five saddle horses, and eight mules, I set out in late May to retrace the previous year's circuitous ride across the foothills and into the high mountains. This year a heavy snowstorm forced us to lay over a day at Quaking Aspen Meadow before proceeding on to the Kern Canyon Ranger Station. We were joined at Quaking Aspen by Leonard Shellenbarger and his wife who were returning to the Mt. Whitney Ranger Station for the summer. With the addition of their horses and mules, we made up a sizable packtrain.

As we had last year, we stopped for the night at Trout Meadow, and arrived at the Kern station the next day, on the afternoon of May twenty-eighth. It was gratifying to be back, and I looked forward to another summer comparable in rewards to the past one. In a few days we put things in shape around the station and vicinity before Shellenbarger and Wren took up their duties elsewhere. At the same time I began my patrols around the district, observing and reporting on snow conditions. In the meantime, far away in another world, in a Superior Court in Los Angeles, a final decree of divorce was entered on June 5, and I was single again.

Ten days later, June 15, Johnny Wren and I rode out to Quaking Aspen to pick up supplies and another man for his trail crew. Alice met us late that afternoon and returned to the station with us the next day. Riding and pack stock that perform hard work in the mountains all summer long need more than the pasturage to be found in meadows to maintain their strength, so I made another trip to Quaking Aspen a few days later to bring in a number of eighty-pound sacks of barley. This I coordinated with the arrival of Dave and Hilda.

I had seen Dave frequently since the days we lived together in 1935. On the other hand, I had seen Hilda only twice in the six years since she terminated our romantic relationship. In the meantime, they had married and were living in Los Angeles where, after graduating from medical school at USC, Dave was interning at the Los Angeles County General Hospital. They both badly needed a respite from the intern grind, so I invited them to take a week's vacation at the Kern Ranger Station. They accepted, and here they were.

En route to the station next day, after we had finished our lunch, Dave discovered that he had lost his wallet. He had had it when we set out that morning, but now it was gone. I wondered if it was worthwhile to make a search for it, which would be a little like looking for a needle in a haystack, so I asked him how much was in it. He replied, "Twenty dollars, all the money we have in the world." That did it. I suggested that they ride on while I turned back to try to find their total earthly substance. We were lucky. In about thirty minutes I saw it lying half buried in the dust at the side of the trail. It must have worked itself out of Dave's back pocket as he rode

ALICE AND JOHNNY WREN

CONTERNO'S STORE AT LEWIS CAMP

along. When I then caught up with them with the good news, they were overjoyed.*

For four of the five days Dave and Hilda were at the cabin in the Kern with Alice and me, I was officially occupied at the station. It was an idyllic period, deep in the enchanting Kern Canyon, the four of us alone, enjoying the best that life can offer. It was with an uneasy sense of loss that I escorted my guests out to Quaking Aspen on June 27, because three of the people who played the largest roles in making my life so full in those Depression years were leaving my company. But I had no time to become lonely, because another friend, Marc Goodnow, a professor of journalism at USC, was at hand to accompany me and my mules back to the Kern station.

Marc stayed with me until July 11, and that is the way it went all summer. There was rarely any appreciable length of time that I was alone, because, as I went out over Farewell Gap or Franklin Pass to Mineral King thereafter for supplies and mail, I was also taking one or two guests out and bringing in others on the return trip. It gave me much pleasure to share the marvelous environment in which I lived with those dear to me. I could not, and did not, let the good times we enjoyed together interfere with my responsibilities, however. There were times when my duties required me to be away from my station for several days. Sometimes my guests would accompany me; most of the time they did not. The latter was the case with Marc when I left him alone at the station while I took off on a four-day patrol.

The Sierra Club, eighty-seven strong, was due to enter my district over Franklin Pass from Mineral King in mid-July for a week's outing. In order to make certain that no problems existed that would interfere with their itinerary, I checked out the area through which they proposed to travel and camp. On

---

*It was an incident that the three of us often reminisced about after Dave became the most successful and sought-after obstetrician in the San Joaquin Valley and later prominent in the field of psychosomatic medicine.

the afternoon of the second day of my patrol, I got into a situation that is frightening to think about even now.

Travel afoot in rugged mountain country is fraught with hazard, and is more so on horseback. There are places where razor-sharp vigilance must be maintained every step of the way, or disaster can result. The lone traveller is especially at risk, because there is no one to help when life is threatened. This was particularly true of the ranger who, early in the season, sometimes had to be away from the nearest communication or human presence for several days at a time. Now, the use of walkie-talkies and helicopters has virtually eliminated the potential for an accident becoming a fatality due to such isolation. But during the days I rangered, this was not the case. There was a job to be done, and mostly we had to do it alone. We depended on a combination of good judgement and good luck to protect us from mishaps.

Several times already this season I had turned back at fords where streams rampaged with waters of the June snow melt. It has never been easy for me to give up on any venture, so I took chances, but when my experience and gut feeling combined to warn me of a strong potential for disaster, I drew the line. On July 7, the scenario was different. It was one wherein a lack of alertness or particular kind of experience, or both, combined to betray me.

I had camped the night before at the Big Arroyo Patrol Station under the brow of the Black Kaweah, some fifteen miles from the Kern station, and on this particular day had tethered my mule there while I rode on up to Kaweah Gap in the morning. After returning to the patrol station for lunch, I proceeded south toward Black Rock Pass, again leaving the mule behind. The Little Five Lakes area was in this direction, and, since the Sierra Club was to camp there for four days, I wanted to check it out.

I was mounted on Queen. She was a mottled gray, sturdy on her feet and strong in sinew, a powerful mare of better-than-average size. She was a prima donna, but ultimately always carried me wherever I wanted to go. When I urged her up a particularly steep section of the trail, one still spotted with perhaps six inches of snow, she responded with characteristic will and determination. The trail here was quite narrow, a sort of trough where my knee brushed lightly against a sheer rock face to my right and my left foot dragged in its stirrup against a thin upheaval of granite on the opposite side. Sure-footed though she was, loose rock on parts of the trail and an icy base underlying the snow on other parts were too much for Queen. She stumbled, regained her balance momentarily, then scrambled wildly in an attempt to retain her footing. But it was a losing battle: her left front and rear feet slipped out from under her, and she began to fall broadside to the left.

I immediately sensed the danger to myself. Queen was falling into a bathtub-like depression whose base was a bit below trail level just beyond the narrow granite ridge that comprised the near side of the tub. My left leg was a split-second away from being crushed by twelve hundred pounds of horseflesh pinning it against the narrow ridge and then rolling over on top of me. What enables a person to survive such a situation is a mind that works with speed that matches an electronic computer in feeding in data and producing a life-saving response.

Just prior to beginning our steep climb up what had become an icy, unstable ladder, we crossed a snowbank that was several feet deep and covered with a light crust, which we had broken through. Reacting instantaneously to the order from my electronic brain, all in one swift motion I lifted my feet from the stirrups, dropped the reins, placed my hands on the pommel of the saddle, and gave myself a mighty push backward, hoping to sail clear of the projecting rocky ledge directly behind me and land on my back in the snowbank five or six feet below.

It worked. The snowbank cushioned my fall like a bed of feathers, and I was unhurt. I climbed back up the trail to find Queen spread-eagled on her back, frantically pawing the air like some gargantuan beetle from a prehistoric world, powerless to rise. I tugged on the reins and coaxed to no avail; the bathtub-like crevice held her in a tight embrace. Thinking out a possible solution to this critical problem I was able to get at the lariat suspended from my saddle and remove it. I then looped one end around Queen's right foreleg, the other end around her right rear leg, and, seeking the best point of leverage for a fulcrum, pulled her toward the trail. Urging her on and timing my heaves at the point of her mightiest exertions, after several attempts I was able to roll her out of the tub and on to her side, whereupon she scrambled unhurt to her feet.

Queen and I emerged from our accident no worse for wear, but we appeared on a stage admirably set for the worst scenario. Had I been pinned with a broken leg or worse under a horse unable to extricate itself from the crevice that cradled us, it requires no fanciful imagination to envision the consequences. There would be great pain, horribly aggravated by a writhing horse, the nocturnal sub-freezing cold at 9,000 feet elevation, the anguished moments when consciousness prevailed, and the ebbing of life under the cruelest of conditions. Not due back to the station for two more days, by the time word got out and searchers were able to find us, who knows how much of our bodies would have disappeared in the maws of carnivorous wild animals.

The next day I rode from the Big Arroyo Patrol Station to the mouth of Soda Creek. The going was rough and my mule lost two shoes en route, so I had to nail on others that afternoon. The trail was seldom used, so I put up signs for the Sierra Club; I didn't want to have to conduct a search for lost hikers in that rough terrain. I also placed signs to indicate the campsite to be used during the club's three-day sojourn here, where convenience and the least adverse impact on the wilderness could be most acceptably combined.

The fourth day out I patrolled up Soda Creek to Little Claire Lake, thence across a rocky bench and on to the top of Franklin Pass at 11,400 feet to assure myself that its crossing would present no problem for the club four days later. From there, I dropped down the trail along Rattlesnake Creek to the Kern Canyon and on along the Kern River to the Kern station, where I arrived after a day of twenty-two hard mountain miles in the saddle.

The following morning I had to put two more shoes on the mule I had taken on the Big Arroyo-Franklin Pass patrol and prepare to leave for Mineral King over Farewell Gap the next day. Terminating his stay, Marc rode out with me on July 11; the next day I met at Mineral King with Oliver Kehrlein, director of the Sierra Club outing, to coordinate our responsibilities. Then, on the 13th, I accompanied the hikers over Franklin Pass to their first night's camp on the shore of Forester Lake. That evening at the campfire, I spoke to the group, outlining their route of travel for the next ten days, noting attractions to be seen, and suggesting side trips from their base camps. Asked to tell a bit about the life of a back-country ranger, I expounded at length on this subject; I had a lot of material on which to draw.

I returned to the Kern station for a few days, then rejoined the Sierra Club at their Soda Creek encampment where I spent two nights and the intervening day with them, making myself useful. It was a friendly and lively group and I enjoyed their company. Among those who made it so pleasant were Dick Leonard, Francis Farquhar, and the leader, Oliver Kehrlein.*

Upon leaving the Sierra Club party at Soda Creek, I headed down the Big Arroyo, up onto the Chagoopa Plateau over a seldom-used trail, and past Moraine Lake and Sky-parlor Meadow to Junction Meadow in the Kern Canyon. Next day, I rode up the Kern-Kaweah Basin to Colby Pass and returned, and the day following to Shepherd Pass via the John Muir Trail to camp that night at Tyndall Creek Cabin. Then came an arduous twenty-four mile patrol from the cabin to Forester Pass on the Kings-Kern Divide via the John Muir

---

*This occasion marked the beginning of my long and increasingly warm friendship with Francis Farquhar, a man I admired and grew truly to appreciate as the mutuality of our interests drew us close together in the later years of his life.

Trail, returning to Junction Meadow by way of Lake South America and the upper Kern Basin. The next evening found me at Lower Funston Meadow where I camped with a convivial party of tourists before returning to the Kern Ranger Station the following morning.

In seven days after having left the Kern Ranger Station, I had ridden one hundred five miles, played host to the Sierra Club, and inspected conditions in the upper part of my district. This patrol was an example of many such I made in a summer's time to keep abreast of what was going on in the area of my responsibility.

I was never happier than on patrol astride a gently rocking horse, plodding leisurely along the trails that veined the magnificently beautiful terrain of the area that I love above all other places on earth. It made little difference which of the many trails I followed through vast forests, alongside resplendent lakes, among wondrous canyons and meadows, across alpine heights bare of all else except shining granite and millions of delicate, many-hued wildflowers, and over high passes that forced a way between snowy summits to reveal far-reaching panoramas. Whatever the route in this region, it invariably produced a sense of gratitude and humility at having the privilege of roaming where only the gods are wont to play. Sequoia National Park has it all—and I knew every hoofstep of every trail, both those well-trodden and those obscure from lack of use for years on end.

In 1941 and 1942, more often than not I rode alone through this enchanting country. With no one to answer to for the quality of my song, I frequently gave voice to the joy that this paradisiacal environment produced in my heart. This could happen anytime and anywhere in the hundreds of miles I travelled on horseback, but one spot in particular seemed to touch the chords in my soul, and I would respond mile after mile at full throat as I ran through my diverse and wide-ranging repertoire until stilled by hoarseness.

The stage for these impromptu concerts (by one who never dared to perform except in solitude) was Rattlesnake Canyon. About half the trips I made between Mineral King, the road-end where I picked up supplies and mail, and my ranger station on the Kern River, were over Franklin Pass on the Great Western Divide that topped out at over 11,000 feet and switchbacked down its eastern approach. At its base one trail turned north to ever-popular Forester Lake while another veered south over little-used Shotgun Pass. It was at this juncture that the terrain opened up into a wide canyon and dropped easily east toward the Kern River for about eight wonder-laden miles before it fell precipitously by switchback into the Kern Canyon.

The south wing of my stage was a long rampart of white granite beautifully mottled in shades of chocolate and orange, rising gracefully hundreds of feet. To the north, along the same distance, lay the overlying rounded brow of a pine-clad ridge. The platform between, which sloped gently down an easy grade, ranged from a quarter-mile to a half-mile in width and was spotted, park-like, with rugged pines. Over all stretched a canopy for which the Sierra Nevada is famous: a cloudless blue vault that reached up into eternity. For my orchestra, I had the purling and bubbling and swishing and rushing of Rattlesnake Creek as it leaped and cascaded and coasted in its play, paralleling my course.

Such moments—and they were countless during my years in Sequoia—were among the very best of my life, and the memories of the ride that I made almost monthly down Rattlesnake Creek during my four summers in the Kern watershed remain with me nearly fifty years later.

The stretch in the Kern Canyon between the ranger station and Junction Meadow was the most heavily travelled in the district, and I needed to take its pulse frequently. One day in mid-August I was camped at Chagoopa Falls Patrol Station when I saw a pillar of smoke rising from near the top of the east rim, opposite my camp; I suspected that it was a fire smoldering from a lightning strike during a thunderstorm a few days before. I did not want it to spread, so I picked up a shovel, an axe, and a mattock and laboriously climbed the steep slope to the fire. It didn't amount to much, but still I had to fight hard for several hours to corral it. That done, I kept a watchful eye on it until a moderate rainfall in the afternoon combined with some hail to extinguish the remaining fingers of flame and live coals.

Just a week after the Chagoopa fire, in response to notices earlier received, I left the park for a week to undergo physical examinations in connection with my applications for a commission. These were conveniently scheduled only a few days apart and were conducted at a minor U. S. Naval Medical Facility in Chavez Ravine (since displaced to make room for the Dodger's Stadium complex in downtown Los Angeles). The location of this late-summer break from the backcountry fortunately gave me an opportunity to make some important personal visits, after which I returned to Sequoia.

Barely back on the job again, I spent the first three days of September looking for a horse that had strayed from a government inspection party in upper Rattlesnake. This was a good example of one way a backcountry ranger gets to know even the most remote sections and seldom-travelled trails in his district. Beginning my search at the top of Rattlesnake Gorge, I rode west up the creek, then south to Shotgun Pass. I then crisscrossed back north over the Rattlesnake Creek watershed to Forester and Little Claire lakes. At the latter lake I turned back south, leaving the trail to cut across country on an extensive elevated bench. Finally I picked my way over new country to Shotgun Pass again, before returning empty-handed over Coyote Pass to the Kern Ranger Station. The errant horse, after hiding out for a week or so, decided to return to domesticated life and was found wandering near a well-travelled trail virtually asking to be picked up.

Not quite a week following my return to the station after scouring the forests and benches of the Rattlesnake watershed, I began a five-day patrol that took me to the summit of Mt. Whitney and back. Although I was confident that section of my district was being well-handled by my assistant at Crabtree Meadow, I wanted to make a personal inspection. Ordinarily I would have done so much earlier, but I had been too occupied with other matters.

The first day I rode up Golden Trout Creek to Tunnel

Ranger Station to conduct liaison with Bruce Morgan, the forest ranger stationed there. I had a lot of time to think along the trail, as I rode alone for hours on end through the mountains. I did a lot of it. Next morning as I headed for Siberian Pass, I mentally reviewed where I stood financially. Having adhered strictly to the plan (made possible by my two summers in the Kern) of setting aside one hundred dollars each month of the one hundred twenty left in my paycheck after meeting my child-support obligation, I would be able to emerge at the close of the season in about six weeks not owing a cent. It was a great relief to have discharged the debt that had begun to accrue only a few days after my ill-fated marriage almost four-and-a-half years before, and burgeoned thereafter, plaguing me all that time. I could not have done it had it not been for the ten months that I lived a simple and spartan life in the backcountry. It was a blessing that I took into account as I balanced the books of my life up to that point. The persistent cloud that hung over my head had finally dissipated.

My reverie was interrupted by the rapid accumulation of clouds of another nature. These appeared above and to the north, the direction in which I was headed. As I reached the top of Siberian Pass, a few flakes of snow began to float haphazardly through the air. The storm quickly gathered momentum, and by the time I dropped down to Rock Creek and followed it to Guyot Pass, it was snowing in earnest. It was a gentle snow, but the flakes were large and falling fast. I became a little alarmed as the snow began to accumulate and obscure the trail as I cleared the pass.

Although I had a sense of the lay of the land, I was in country that I did not know well. However, the forest through which I passed was an open one, and I managed to make out signs of the trail and follow its dim outline to Crabtree Meadow. It was with considerable relief that, with three or four inches of snow atop the pack on my mule, I rode up to the ranger cabin from whose cozy warmth the Shellenbargers came out to welcome me, obviously themselves relieved that I had arrived safely after my day's journey of twenty-seven miles.

The storm wore itself out sometime during the night, and the day dawned brittle and clear with five inches of snow on the ground at the Mt. Whitney Ranger Station. It was an early-fall forerunner that presaged the winter that would soon set in in the high county. Although the snow had drifted up to two feet along some parts of the trail, I was able to pick my way around the deepest drifts and reach the top of Mt. Whitney, whose summit was covered by ten inches of fresh snow; for vast distances in three directions, the land was covered with a blanket of pristine white. The east was an exception, where the Owens Valley spread out far and wide in dun colors, mottled by the Alabama Hills and the little town of Lone Pine in the depths immediately below.

After my return two days later to the Kern Ranger Station, I began an inspection circuit of the trails that descended into the Kern Canyon and those that rose off the Chagoopa Plateau to the high passes of the Great Western Divide, in order to install and clear turnouts that would reduce damage from winter storm runoff. It was during this period that I received official notice of the results of my physical examinations in Los Angeles. The U. S. Navy informed me that I was ineligible for a naval commission because I was underweight. This didn't disturb me as in the same mail the U.S. Army Air Corps advised me that I had passed the physical and was a successful applicant for a commission as a first lieutenant in counter-sabotage. I was requested to stand by and await orders to report for duty. I was delighted. My joy was short-lived, however, because a short time later I received another letter which informed that all direct procurement of officers for the Army Air Corps had been cut off. So that also had come to a dead end. I had no choice but to accept these unhappy developments for the present and concentrate on completing my season's work in the Kern.

The time was at hand when I had to ride out and drop pasture and drift fences to prevent their breaking during the heavy winter snows. Finally, there was the park boundary to patrol during the hunting season. By the time I closed the station and rode out over Coyote Pass and Farewell Gap to Mineral King late in October, I had logged thirteen hundred miles on horseback for the summer and deposited in my memory bank a wealth of rewarding experiences.

Once back at Ash Mountain I felt good in the knowledge that at last my personal problems had been solved and I was again a free man on all counts. On the other hand, the world was being torn to pieces in a great war, and I still was not helping to solve that problem. Early in the year I had registered with my local draft board as required by law. I had been placed in Category 3-A because I had a dependent. I had not been called up, nor was there much of a prospect that I would be in the near future.

I had no clear idea of what direction I wanted to take when I came out of the Kern. I did know that I wanted to get my show on the road. I still wanted a commission, and if I couldn't get it one way, I'd try another. Thus it was that I went to Fresno and took the qualifying test for Volunteer Officer Candidate (VOC) status, which would assure me assignment to an officer candidate school (OCS) upon completion of army basic training. I passed, but held off actually signing up while I explored alternatives.

Flying appealed to me, but I was too old to become a fighter pilot. I looked into the Civil Air Patrol program and became mildly interested, but this provided instruction only and no pay. This meant I would have to support myself during the training period. I had no money for that and would be without an income for at least three months. That was more than I could handle financially, so I dropped the idea.

I then made a trip to San Francisco Bay area. The best I could do was a possible assignment as a non-commissioned officer working in plain clothes as a Counter-Intelligence Corps agent. This was not quite what I had in mind many months ago, but I had reached a point where it appeared to be a pretty good deal. I left the Presidio with the assurance of the CIC commandant that he wanted me and would get the ball rolling. I thought my problem was solved. Not so. A few weeks later I received a letter from the CIC commandant, advising me that a hitch had developed in bringing me into his office. He wrote that he still wanted me and asked me to be patient for a period of time whose length he could not foretell, until the problem could be solved.

I could be patient no longer. The world was in flames, while I sat on the sidelines safe and secure in my isolated mountain retreat—without challenge or purpose. I had tried at some length to direct my own military destiny, but nothing had worked out. Enough was enough. I didn't even take the time to go ahead with further processing of my VOC application. I simply notified my draft board that I was volunteering for immediate induction into the U.S. Army. I would take my chances, come what may, and contribute to the war effort to the best of my ability by whatever means would develop.

The draft board did not dilly-dally. I was notified to appear in Fresno on November 30 to be sworn into service. I had already made the decision to sell my automobile. It would be useless to me for a long time to come—in truth, an impediment. It was not easy to give up this fine little vehicle, which had been such a solace to me during bad times. It was almost as much a part of me as an arm or a leg. If one can feel affection for a mechanical object, I did for my faithful companion, that sporty little Chevy. Reluctantly, I sold it, but retained possession until I went on active duty.

After being sworn in, I was given seven-days leave to settle my affairs before reporting for active duty at the Presidio of Monterey on December 7, 1942, exactly one year after the Pearl Harbor catastrophe. I gathered my scanty possessions together, stored a few with friends in Exeter, and left the remainder with my mother in Santa Monica. I spent some time with my son, but it was with Alice that I passed most of that week. It was a bittersweet time. I think we both had a premonition that this would be the end of our relationship, although it was never openly discussed. Alice was a splendid human being, one who had meant so much to me at a crisis in my life, and I had given some thought to asking her to marry me. Somehow, though, that last spark needed to move me failed to materialize.

At last the day came when Private Wallace, U.S. Army, climbed on a small bus at Exeter, some twenty-five miles from Ash Mountain. There were about a dozen of us aboard this Monterey-bound vehicle, all from the area, headed for diverse and unknown fates. I was thirty-three, single, and in perfect health. I owed no one and had a check for two hundred fifty dollars in my pocket, derived from the sale of my automobile. An era in my life had ended and a new one was beginning. I looked forward to it with excitement.

8

In the Wake of the War

The war years were good to me. By the time I returned to Sequoia after an absence of almost forty months, I had undergone extensive training as an infantryman at Camp Chaffee, Arkansas, and Camp Pickett, Virginia; pursued Far Eastern and Japanese studies for six months at Yale University; and played a part in what has been called the greatest battle ever fought by an American army—the Battle of the Bulge. I had travelled east of the Mississippi River for the first time and had seen something of England, Scotland, France, Belgium, the Netherlands, and Germany. I spent five wonderful days and nights in Paris, the city of my dreams, as well as visiting the great European capitals of Brussels and London. Best of all, I found Mary, who became my war bride and was with me not only in New Haven and Virginia, but also in Ann Arbor where the U.S. Army sent me to the University of Michigan to continue my studies in the Japanese language for nine more months following my service in Europe.

After the surrenders of Germany and Japan, I was discharged at Fort Custer, Michigan, on November 22, 1945. Thanks to Superintendent John R. White, who graciously extended my military furlough for the purpose, I was able to complete studies as a civilian at Ann Arbor, which earned me a Bachelor of Arts degree from the university in the field of Oriental Language and Literature, with a major in Japanese.

Although those years were rich indeed, I eagerly looked forward to the time I could return to Sequoia and resume my park service career. Hence it was with great pleasure that former Sergeant Wallace reported to the chief ranger at Ash Mountain Headquarters on March 16, 1946, with a lovely new wife as a helpmate.

Kings Canyon National Park had been established in 1940, and during the war it was combined with Sequoia National Park under one administration. Thus it was that the assignment to Grant Grove that I received upon my return was beyond the bounds of my former duty stations but within the now-combined parks.

The Generals Highway between the parks was closed because of deep snow when Mary and I set out for Grant Grove in Kings Canyon National Park a few days later. Hence we had to drop down into the San Joaquin Valley at Woodlake and gradually climb north through the foothills. The weather was unsettled to begin with, and after we left the valley snow began to fall. We struggled on as far as Pinehurst, but snow on the road and in the air made it impossible to travel any farther. We sought shelter on the outskirts of town and luckily found a middle-aged couple with a spare bedroom in their house, and they took us in.

The storm abated during the night, and by the time we left Pinehurst in the morning, the road had been cleared up into Grant Grove six miles away. The quarters we were assigned were only about two hundred yards from the village center, so we were able to move in without too much trouble. Indeed this was no problem, because the sturdy Plymouth Town Sedan that we had bought in Ann Arbor to take us west carried our entire worldly possessions. Ours was a relatively new six-room residence, well-enough furnished, all things considered. We were both pleased with it, and looked forward to having this as our home for the foreseeable future.

We were barely settled in when it began to snow again. It snowed and snowed and snowed with little interruption for almost a week. By the time this late-March storm dissipated, there was six feet of white stuff on the level. In fact, the path I had to shovel between our porch and the roadway became an open trench deep enough to enclose my entire upright body. Of course this scene constituted a Sierra winter wonderland, made even more other-worldly by our isolation. It was not a new experience for me, but for Mary it was a revelation. She had never been deep in the mountains before, nor had she ever known a scene as pristine and soul-stirring. She was overwhelmed, and I was gratified because the glorious pictures I had painted about what we would share in my beloved Sierra Nevada had been proven to be no idle boast.

I was completely content at Grant Grove; this was what I had lived through the war years to return to. I was proud to be a park ranger, and I let the world know about it by putting "Ranger" before my name on the return address of all my correspondence. It was a title I held as worthy as any in professional and military walks of life. Grant Grove had become my special charge, and I set about at once to shape it up to my standards before the tourist season got underway in earnest and the campgrounds began to fill up.

I began the sweep of my new broom at the little one-room building at the center of Grant Grove Village, which doubled as my office and the off-season information center. I scrubbed the walls and floor, washed the windows, did some painting, and reorganized the handling of information for visitors. Since maintenance crews were not yet available, I also cleaned the toilets, collected the trash, and literally swept the streets around the office and village coffee-shop with a push broom. In good time all was in order, and I was eager to meet the surge of a visiting public and help them to enjoy their stay in my domain. I expected to have a crew of temporary rangers to help me get the job done in the best possible way. It looked as if a great summer was in the offing.

My duties at Grant Grove were temporarily suspended early in May while I attended a combined fire training and ranger conference at Port Angeles, Washington, headquarters of Olympic National Park. Eighteen of us were selected for this week-long meeting. Ten national parks and monuments in the West were represented by various superintendents, custodians, chief rangers, and rangers. Additionally, there were personnel from the Director's Office and the Region Four Office. As the Sequoia-Kings Canyon National Park representatives, Chief Ranger John Wegner, Ranger Stanley Bechtel, and I drove up and back in a government vehicle, a legitimate travel bonus we all enjoyed.

I was assigned to make a presentation having to do with "Park Rangers and the Winter Programs." In my talk, I advanced two basic concepts for consideration and discussion: (1) how to shift a part of the burgeoning summer travel load to the winter months, and (2) the advisability of setting up a winter sports training program for members of the ranger force. All in all, I thought the week well-spent and was pleased to have been able to participate. It appeared that I was on the right track.

Then the blow fell. After only two months at Grant Grove, I was suddenly pulled out and returned to the Kern Ranger Station. I was deeply disappointed. Considered in the light of efficient administration and protection of the parks, I could not quarrel with that decision. After all, I was better qualified to handle affairs in the Kern Canyon-Mt. Whitney area than anyone else. But by the same token I could be buried in the Kern for years to come. Viewed subjectively this move was a step backward. My position at Grant Grove had potential for career advancement, and that was now the name of my game. However, I had no choice in the matter, and I did as I was instructed. The assignment was highly desirable per se. It was a post that many would have given a right arm to hold, but it offered me no further challenges. Thus it was that Mary and I gave up our happy home at Grant Grove and made ready to migrate to the Kern Canyon.

In contrast to pre-war years, we did not have to make the

circuitous eighty-five mile ride from Ash Mountain to Kern Ranger Station. Stock, equipment, and supplies were trucked to Quaking Aspen Meadow on May 21, and Mary and I rode out from there on May 24, after a two-day layover due to snow and bad weather. In addition to the two of us there were Jim, Eddie, Shorty, Susy, Sam, and Kitten to share the summer with us. Jim was my saddle horse, Eddie was Mary's, and the others were temperamental, long-eared beasts of burden. There was no trail crew.

Mary had never ridden a horse before, so we chose to break the twenty-six mile ride to the Kern Ranger Station with an overnight stop at Trout Meadow, fourteen miles out of Quaking Aspen. The next day we rode on to the station, where I received the shock of my life. The cabin, inside and out, and the acre of ground surrounding it were the scene of such filth and disarray that I wondered if I was back in some war-torn German village. I was outraged. Before going off to war more than three years before, I had left this station in an immaculate condition. What I now found could not have been worse. The most repugnant feature of it all was what confronted my wife in lieu of the wonderful mountain home I had previously described to her.

My first impulse was to turn right around and ride back to Quaking Aspen the next morning. I would demand that a crew be sent out to clean up the mess before I would return with my wife. I was prepared to resign if this was not done. However, after sleeping on the matter overnight, I took a less emotional, more commonsense view. The problem was there, and it had to be handled. As the ranger back in charge of the district, I had inherited a mess, but it was up to me as the man on the spot to clean it up. I talked it over with Mary, and we decided to stay on. It was a lot to ask any woman to do, but she, always a good sport, pitched in to help. We worked hard and long for three full days before we got things in good shape.

Before we started the cleanup I made a detailed record, item by item, of all that was wrong. After the renovation, my first order of business was to sit down and write a memorandum to the superintendent through the chief ranger. It was a scathing report, three pages long, in which I laid out every detail and minced no words in my denunciation, letting the chips fall where they may.

Within a week, Superintendent White replied with a memorandum to me, through the chief ranger, which was conciliatory in nature. He advanced several plausible reasons how the situation I found could have developed. Among them was the virtual abandonment of the district by permanent rangers during the war, except for one too chronically ill to do the job; the necessity to make frequent changes in temporary personnel who occupied the station most of the time; and the short tours of duty that began late in the season and ended early in the fall, thus exposing the cabin to vandalism. He offered me every assistance within the limitation of park appropriations to improve conditions in the district and expressed the desire to make the Kern-Mt. Whitney District my permanent assignment. Finally, a person of real class that I knew him to be, he expressed his regrets to Mary for the mess with which she'd had to contend.

Although I did not think the explanations given by the colonel entirely covered the situation, still I believed that it did in his view, considering the information that was probably given to him at headquarters after a short investigation. It all boiled down to the fact that my old home, if not the district as a whole, had become a casualty of war—and I was the one who had to heal it. I liked the colonel a lot; he had always treated me right, and I accepted his memo in the same good faith in which it was written and set about justifying his expression of confidence that the district was again in good hands.

The good colonel might have had second thoughts about me, though, had he been aware of an incident that took place on my fifth day back in the canyon. I had never ridden Eddie, the small but wiry bay that had been assigned as Mary's mount, so I thought he and I ought to get acquainted. It was an easy, pleasant ride some three miles down the river to

Little Kern Lake, so I saddled up Eddie and down the trail we

MARY AND EDDIE

went, just the two of us. It was after we reached the lake and turned back that I came close to getting killed.

There was a level grassy area in which grew a clump of quaking aspen alongside a backwater of the lake. It was almost two hundred yards long and about a hundred feet wide. The trail that wound through this glade in gently sweeping curves was free of rock, so I did what came naturally to me. There was no reason for a running horse to stumble racing through this stretch, and a tight rein could keep it on the trail and out of the trees. I knew, because I had done this here many times through two summers just before the war. It was one of the rare opportunities to really cut loose in these mountains, and I never missed taking advantage when my duties brought me through here without a pack animal or two in tow.

As I neared the level area, I loosened the reins a bit and kicked Eddie in the ribs. We flew along the trail, our speed accelerating. Then, for a moment, I unaccountably relaxed my control. No sooner did Eddie feel the tension go out of the reins than he veered off the trail and headed through the little grove of quaking aspen. I tried to rein him back to the trail, but he prevailed in his hell-bent course. I then tried to rein him in to a slower gait or a stop, but there was no way; he was too strong for me. I knew I was in big trouble, because now he had his head. All I could do was to hang on and hope for the best.

At this point Eddie set a collision course for an eight-inch quaking aspen no more than fifty feet ahead. Reining now was an exercise in futility. Eddie gave no sign at all of any intention other than to crash the two of us into that tree at full speed. I thought I knew horses well enough to be certain they are not given to committing suicide. Working with that premise, I had to believe this horse was going to dodge that aspen at the last split second before impact. This being the case, I felt I had two options. One was to guess which side of the tree Eddie would swerve to, then lean far from the saddle in the direction of that swerve, and thus miss the tree and injury as Eddie brushed by its side. Of course if I guessed wrong and Eddie went to the opposite side of the tree, my lean would take me head-on into the tree with almost certainly fatal consequences. My other option was to stick in the saddle like a burr, tensed with all my strength in an effort to remain upright with Eddie whichever way he went and hope for the best, knowing that the momentum of the swerve was bound to throw me against the tree to some extent.

It was a hard choice, and it had to be made in a flash. Again I experienced the marvel that is the mind of man in an emergency. The answer came to me quickly; it was to not gamble with my life, to take my loss whatever it might be and to let it go at that. Accordingly, I remained tensely upright, and Eddie's swerve brought me a glancing blow against one side of the tree. The impact drove me in a somersault over the rear of my horse, and I landed full on my back, the wind knocked completely out of me.

I lay on the ground fighting for air and feeling as if I had been destroyed. My breath returned eventually, but I didn't move. I was afraid of finding some of my bones broken. Still lying on my back, I moved one leg—it was okay. Then I moved the other—it too responded normally. Then I tried an arm—no problem. Finally I raised the other arm—great, both arms and legs okay for sure.

When I got to my feet, I caught sight of Eddie standing a few yards away, reins on the ground, the epitome of innocence and eyeing me as if to ask, "Is there any stupidity to which man will not descend?" But he permitted me to climb aboard, and calmly took me back to the cabin. There I dismounted and collapsed on the front porch.

Mary was stunned. Here this husband of hers, who was supposed to be at home in the mountains, had brought her into this vast wilderness, and, in less than a week after arriving, had shown that he couldn't even take care of himself, not to mention her. But she adjusted quickly, unsaddled Eddie, took him to the pasture, and returned to do what she could for me. It was ludicrous, the tenderfoot ministering to this old-timer who, although he hadn't shot himself in the foot, had done something almost equally as foolish. Unscathed during the recent war, it was ironic that I accomplished on my own home grounds what Hitler's Wehrmacht had failed to do on the battlefield.

I did not rise from my cot for almost twenty-four hours. I felt as if I had been hit by a ten-ton truck. I guess I might just as well have been. My impact against the tree had driven my right elbow into my lower ribs on that side, breaking three of them (I learned this a month later). I had been warmly dressed due to the high elevation and the earliness of the season, but the brush against the tree had torn my leather jacket, shredded my woolen G.I. sweater, split my woolen G.I. shirt, and peeled off more than a square inch of skin under my longjohns, all at the elbow. The tree itself did not emerge unscathed, a later investigation revealed. Its bark at the point of impact had been neatly and completely peeled off in the shape of a disk about five inches in diameter.

It was a lot easier to forgive Eddie than it was to forgive myself. It was a close call. I had carelessly lost control at a site many miles and hours removed from medical attention. My ribs healed naturally, but it was some time before I could swing an axe or lift a weight without pain. It was a lesson learned the hard way—one that helped me survive several thousand miles more on horseback in the mountains. I also had Mary with me for most of those miles; she had rapidly become an accomplished horsewoman and on our many patrols together kept me on an even keel.

There was a lot of work to be done to prepare for the season's travel into the district, so I went about doing it for the next month. I set up trail registers at the Kern Canyon, Golden Trout Creek, and Coyote Pass entrances to the park; worked trails to Coyote Pass and up the canyon to Kern Hot Springs, where I put up the fence and cleaned out the bathhouse and spring; maintained the telephone from Kern Ranger Station to Chagoopa Patrol Station and up to Coyote Pass. I also put up fences on both sides of the canyon as far as Rock Creek. At the station between these tasks, I cleaned out the cesspool, built feeding boxes for stock, rebuilt the barley box, dug a new garbage pit, cleaned and sorted tools, erected a flagpole, shod several head of stock, cleaned up the grounds, and chopped wood.

Among my responsibilities early in the season was the acquisition of first-hand information about snow depths and the condition of passes in the high country; this meant making patrols as far as I could get on horseback into the upper elevations of the district. A good example was my first one of the year that occurred on June 6, when I rode from the Kern Ranger Station to the foot of Franklin Pass. I found the trail in Rattlesnake Gorge and upper Rattlesnake Canyon badly washed out and the snow from twelve to eighteen inches deep in the meadow at the foot of the pass. This kind of information was important to headquarters in the planning of trail maintenance and in responding to inquiries about accessibility. It also supplemented the measurement of snow survey crews with respect to what growers in the San Joaquin Valley could figure on with regard to water runoff. This particular patrol was especially memorable in that the thirty-two miles covered was the longest single-day ride I ever made in the mountains, and it was made just exactly one week after Eddie had helped me crack three ribs. But then, backcountry rangers are a tough breed; they have to be to get the job done, come what may.

Also during this period, Mary and I made a five-day, eighty-mile round trip ride to Atwell Mill Ranger Station for supplies. En route, I put up the twenty-two miles of telephone line from Coyote Pass across the Little Kern watershed to Quinn Horse Camp and on to Hockett Meadow Ranger Station. This established direct telephone communication between Kern Ranger Station and Ash Mountain headquarters, as I found the line to be open between Hockett Meadow and Atwell Mill.

On June 26, Ray Buckman and Bill Neelands came into the canyon to open up the Lewis Camp store. Jules Conterno had died during the war, and Mae was not up to handling the business alone, so Ray had taken over this operation. It fit in well with his enterprises in Mineral King, where he now owned and operated both the pack station and store. William Neelands had also passed away during the war; Bill, in his early twenties, was his son and with his mother Lucia managed the Lewis Camp business for Ray for several summers.

Visitors required very little of my attention during the month of June, since only thirty-seven people and thirty-six head of stock were recorded. July was a different story, as five hundred thirty-five people and sixty-eight head of stock were registered. By the first of that month I had acquired a trail crew and by mid-July, a temporary ranger, to assist me. This was a godsend, for in August, 1,490 people and 1,892 head of stock were registered at the various entrances to the Kern District—and this did not include those who ascended Mt. Whitney from the Owens Valley side, or those who failed to register. The trail crew was able to work the high passes just ahead of this influx to make the trails passable and even improve a few to some extent. Furthermore, after that the temporary ranger stationed at the Mt. Whitney Ranger Station controlled the visitors in the north end of the district.

The Sierra Club was quite active in the district during July. A saddle party of forty-four, with thirty-one pack animals, entered the park through the Kern Ranger Station entrance on June 28, en route to Little Whitney Meadow. On July 1, this group again entered the park via Siberian Pass to camp in Rock Creek before returning over the pass to the Kern Plateau. This party required little attention as it barely touched the park.

Another much larger group was soon due that would focus on Mt. Whitney. Inasmuch as I did not yet have an assistant at the Mt. Whitney Ranger Station, I rode in there on July 5 and put up a small pasture fence near the station, then spent the following two days cleaning up the cabin and grounds. I then rode over into Rock Creek and up to Army Pass on July 9 to make contact with a Sierra Club hiking party of one hundred twenty hikers and seventy head of stock. That evening I talked to the group at their campfire about what to see in the country they were headed for, and, on the following day, doubled back to Mt. Whitney Ranger Station.

Since the Sierra Club hikers were due at the Mt. Whitney Ranger Station to camp in the area for three days, I patrolled to the summit of Mt. Whitney on July 12, working the trail as I went to make sure it was passable and safe for those who would try for the top. After the group arrived the next day, I stayed with them to cover possible emergencies until they moved on north up the John Muir Trail on July 16. I then returned to Kern Ranger Station via Siberian Pass, Tunnel Ranger Station, and Golden Trout Creek.

On July 19 I got some valuable help when Temporary Ranger Richard Hester reported for duty at the Kern Ranger Station. I briefed Hester on his responsibilities at Mt. Whitney Ranger Station and environs, the station and area he was to look after; made out tentative work plans and schedules; and sent him on his way to his new home at the base of Mt. Whitney a few days later. But before he got away, I took advantage of my first help of the season to put him on the other end of a crosscut saw, helping me work up a good bit of firewood for the station.

In late July, I rode into Mineral King for supplies and returned the next day. At the same time, Chief Ranger John Wegner had ridden out the High Sierra Trail from the Wolverton Corrals on an inspection trip. He called me from Junction Meadow to remind me of the survey to be made by Fred Paget, senior hydraulic engineer for the State of California's Department of Public Works. He then went on to the summit of Mt. Whitney before heading north over Forester Pass into the Kings Canyon country in early August.

I had already been alerted in writing about the Paget visit. Thus I rode up Golden Trout Creek to Big Whitney Meadow the next day where I met the Paget party. With Mr. Paget were E. H. Hyatt, state engineer, State of California; Roy L. May, engineer for the Tulare County Storage District; and Mr. Van Horton, a civil engineer from Paget's office. They were there to conduct a survey of the Kern Plateau to select cabin sites for snow-gauging purposes. Inasmuch as these cabins could be made available to park service personnel on patrol, it was my cue to assist in selection of sites in such a manner as would be most advantageous to the park.

Early that evening I received information that a fire was burning near the Kern Ranger Station. Presumably it had originated from a lightning strike earlier that day. I had no choice but to return to the Kern Ranger Station at once, so I left the Big Whitney camp at nine o'clock. Since my instructions from Superintendent White were to accompany the Paget party through the district if possible, I got in touch with Ranger Hester and asked him to meet the party in Rock Creek next day and take over my role. It was three o'clock in the morning when I finally arrived at the Kern Ranger Station, to complete thirty miles in the saddle that day.

Sure enough, early next afternoon I spotted a small cloud of smoke rising from a point perhaps a quarter-mile north of the park boundary along Coyote Creek and about the same distance above the Kern Ranger Station. It was too close to bother with stock, so I picked up tools from the station fire cache and climbed to it afoot. The fire had done very little damage, as it was mostly confined to the ground in an open, park-like area. The tree that had been struck was the only casualty so far, but the ground fire presented a danger to the many fine, full-grown western yellow pines that flourished here. Alternately using a shovel and mattock, I tried to establish a fire line around it. I got three sides well-corralled, but the side on which the fire was advancing was another matter.

I shovelled and grubbed furiously, pausing only to race from one point to another where the flames were creeping more rapidly through the grass and low-lying brush. I would attack that point, only to have another point take up the gauntlet and fling it at me with fiery fingers. I was busier than the proverbial one-armed paper hanger. In fact, I drove myself to the limit, as I was determined to get control of the fire. The battle went on and on, as I refused to give up. Finally, gasping for breath, no longer able to lift a tool, my legs wobbling underneath me, I dropped in my tracks at the side of the advancing fire, too exhausted to do other than lie there. It was about twenty minutes before I regained enough strength to get to my feet. Meanwhile, the fire crept merrily and inexorably along the ground. It had been an uneven battle. Nature had once more vanquished puny man. So I said, "the hell with it," and hoped it would burn itself out that night.

The fire was out when I checked it next morning, so I prepared to rejoin the Paget party at once. However, on my journey up the canyon later that day, headed for another rendezvous with Paget, I spotted a fire on Rattlesnake Point close to the canyon rim, well off the trail above Rattlesnake Gorge. The fire had first priority on my services, so again I was frustrated in my efforts personally to work with Mr. Paget and his companions, although they were in good hands with Ranger Hester.

The site was well-nigh inaccessible to stock, but I carefully picked my way to it, guided by its smoke. When I arrived I found an entirely different situation there than the afternoon before. An acre had already been blackened. Several down logs, from twelve to eighteen inches in diameter, were blazing away and tongues of fire were slowly licking up the sides of the few trees still standing. There were hot coals all over the place, and outside the fire's perimeter was a tangled mass of brush and young growth. I found a safe place to unpack and tie up my horse and mule and decided the only thing I could do was to let it burn itself out while trying to keep it from spotting outside the area already burned. Since the area was fairly rocky and there was little grass, ground fire was not a problem. Thus I had no real trouble confining the fire to the area already scourged. Nonetheless, I felt I had to keep watch all night to make sure that if a blazing cone or limb or small ember fell outside the burn, I would be on hand to snuff it out. By putting myself in that position, I witnessed a sight that banished my fatigue and lifted me into another realm.

In writing about a night fire he chanced upon in the forest between the Middle and East forks of the Kaweah, John Muir has described what I saw as "strange wild fireworks, too beautiful and exciting to allow much sleep." He refers to

143

"great fallen trunks lying on the hillsides all red and glowing like colossal iron bars fresh from a furnace . . . overspread with a pure, rich, furred, ruby glow almost flameless and smokeless, producing a marvelous effect in the night." What I felt, however, was even more stirring than this resplendent sight. There, alone in the dark of night, far from any evidence of man and his works, the emanations from the logs, shot through with a gently pulsating, velvety rich red glow, warm and smokeless, mesmerized me. This raised me from a worldly to an ethereal plane where I felt in tune with cosmic forces. This transcendence was a totally spiritual experience, remarkably born out of a lightning-ignited fire on the rim of the Kern Canyon.

Fascinated, I watched the flickering flames and throbbing coals all night, taking time off now and then to keep the burn under control. All the next day I fought it until, piece by piece, it surrendered. To confirm my physical conquest, I stayed over another night to make sure the fire was dead. But when I left there that morning, it was with the strong feeling that in a spiritual sense it was I who had been overcome.

I still had hopes of catching up with the Paget party before it left the park, so I struck out for the nearest trail. This happened to be the seldom-used Willow Cutoff. I followed this down the Big Arroyo to its junction with the old U.S. Forest Service trail that climbed abruptly up the north wall of that big cleft in the earth over an almost-obliterated, hazardous path onto the Chagoopa Plateau. Then it was on past Moraine Lake and Skyparlor Meadow to join the High Sierra Trail and drop into the Kern Canyon at Upper Funston Meadow.

The next day I rode from my overnight camp at the Chagoopa Ranger Station on up the canyon past Junction Meadow to strike the Tyndall Creek Trail, which I took up to its junction with the John Muir Trail. This is where I finally caught up with Ranger Hester and the Paget party. That evening Mr. Paget and I had a long discussion during which he outlined certain conclusions developed as a result of his survey, and I advanced my ideas for consideration in the few instances where our minds did not meet. The next day, August 4, I escorted Mr. Paget and his companions to the top of Forester Pass where they crossed into the Kings Canyon country. Later I submitted a three-page memorandum to the chief ranger to inform him of the details of Paget's survey and of the discussion between the two of us.

After leaving Forester Pass, I patrolled to Sheperd Pass, still another high pass on the Sierra crest leading up from the Owens Valley, to place a trail register. From there I doubled back to explore the Bighorn Plateau, ride down the Upper Kern past Lake South America to Junction Meadow, head up into the Kern-Kaweah Basin to Colby Pass and return, and finally ease back down the Kern Canyon to Lewis Camp. In the seven days since leaving the site of the fire on Rattlesnake Point, I had covered one hundred sixteen miles over some of the most rugged and bewitching trails to be found in the High Sierra.

This kind of travel over rough mountain trails is hard on horseshoes and muleshoes. Since leaving the fire at Rattlesnake Point, I had replaced three shoes on my saddle horse and four on my two pack mules. Upon my return to the station, I put three more on the mules. This is the way it went all summer. Since I was much too far away from the government farrier at Wolverton to take advantage of his services, I was on my own. Practice make perfect; replacing a total of sixteen horseshoes and sixteen muleshoes by the season's end kept the skill I had developed in previous summers in the backcountry up to speed. When one considers that the horse and the mule were absolutely essential to proper protection of a vast area such as was under my jurisdiction, it is obvious that it was of prime importance to keep the stock well-fed and well-shod. Without them ready, willing, and able to help do the job, a ranger in the backcountry in that era would have been only half a ranger.

There is a lofty mass of granite called Tower Rock that rises precipitously some fifteen hundred feet just across the Kern River from the ranger station. It is a bastion that guards the southern entrance to the park. Since I always slept on the cabin porch, which faced to the east, it was the first thing I saw in the morning and the last thing I saw at night. For almost three summers, it had challenged me to scale it. Finally I could stand it no longer and set out in late August to get that monkey off my back. It was an arduous but not particularly difficult ascent. I was not a technical rock climber, so the minimal amount of exposure I encountered gave me all the thrill I wanted. Using great care in places where a slip would have been disastrous, I reached the top without incident.

The view was astounding. In the center, far below, dwarfed, reposed the meadow that served as the ranger pasture at Lewis Camp. Opposite, Coyote Creek twisted its way through a heavily forested drainage that culminated at Coyote Pass on the western horizon. South, the canyon walls dwindled rapidly to expose the Little Kern Lakes, while to the north, Little Funston Meadow came into view before the river completely disappeared in the canyon's great cleft. As the eye rose above the unseen river farther on, first Rattlesnake Point, then the mouth of the Big Arroyo, came into view. Beyond and above them, a great unbroken forest carpeted the entire expanse on the western side of the river. Far in the distance, the Chagoopa Plateau led gradually to the mighty Kaweahs on the northern skyline. To the rear, on the east, the terrain rose gently, supporting a vast expanse of rock and tree. It was in the depths of this latter, the Golden Trout Creek watershed, that I found my way to a sight, different in nature, but equally, if not more, captivating than the view from the top.

I'm not sure how it had come to my attention that there was a magnificent gorge through which Golden Trout Creek plunged in its run from the level of Little Whitney Meadow to the sandy flat it crossed just before merging with the waters of the Kern River. Perhaps I had heard about it from someone who had explored it; perhaps I had read about it in some obscure mountain literature. Certainly, few had ever seen it. I had travelled the trail between the Kern Ranger Station and Little Whitney Meadow many times, but always with stock, so I could only wonder what lay somewhat north of the trail that switchbacked so steeply into the Kern. At last afoot, here was a chance to make my own exploration of the Golden Trout Gorge.

The trail crossed Golden Trout Creek from the north side to the south a short distance from Little Whitney Meadow, and it was somewhat below here that I left the trail after having made my way across country from Tower Rock. The going along the creek was easy enough for a spell, but the verdure grew more dense as I gradually dropped down along the now-cascading waters. It was difficult to find a path, but the roar of a mighty unseen falls lured me on. I reached its brink and saw below an enchanting dell that abounded in huge green ferns, a large effervescing pool of water at its center. I simply had to get down to it and savor it at first hand, so I half-slid, half-fell down the side of the falls till I came to rest in this magical spot. The forest that surrounded me here was so dense as to virtually shut out the sky, thus better to hide in its fastness this marvelous work of nature. I felt truly blessed to have joined the few who had wandered into this fairyland.

I was loath to leave, but the afternoon was waning and I had to get out of this gorge. I could see that the creek continued to plunge through even rougher country below the pool. I was alone, so it didn't make sense to push my luck any farther. Furthermore, it would be difficult enough to climb out of the hole I was in. After three or four false starts, I found my way up and out, but not without moments of fright as I came to what seemed a precarious deadend. Once above the falls, however, I struck out south on a contour through the forest until I came to the trail, which I followed on down to the bottom of the hill and across the Kern River suspension bridge to the ranger station. It had been a great day of exploration and adventure, of a kind that in its diversity and grandeur makes life so wonderfully worth living.

Three days later, I was working on my monthly report at the station when the phone rang about four-thirty in the afternoon. It was two long, two short—my call—so I answered.

A stranger who said his name was Sam Siegel was on the line. He was calling from the emergency phone at Junction Meadow. He explained that he and two brothers, Bill and Mark Tuttle, had been backpacking down the John Muir Trail and had made camp at Wallace Lake night before last. Next day, Sam and Bill had climbed nearby Mt. Carillon. In mid-afternoon, on the way back to camp, Bill decided to climb Mt. Russell. This meant a detour and a stiff climb, so Sam, not feeling up to it, had waited while Bill made the ascent. Although not an experienced climber, neither was Bill a novice in the backcountry, as he had been in this region on several occasions. Bill had not returned by dark, so Sam went on back to their camp.

That night Mark and Sam became alarmed when Bill failed to show up. They slept fitfully, hoping to hear him come in, but he didn't. Early next morning, they had made a search in the vicinity of Mt. Russell, but could find no trace of Bill. About one-thirty they decided to solicit aid and had hiked down to Junction Meadow to do so. I suggested to Sam that he and Mark remain at their Wallace Lake camp and told him that I'd get help on the way at once.

The first thing I did was to get in touch with District Ranger Joe Thornton of the Inyo National Forest at Lone Pine, the destination of these three men in a few days, to see if Bill had somehow come on into town. Thornton said he would check all the hotels and the bus station and send a man up to Whitney Portal to check there and with the crew working on the road. By chance, Ranger Hester was with me at the Kern Ranger Station at the time. We agreed that he should proceed without delay to the Wallace Lake camp, which was about ten miles from his duty station at the foot of Mt. Whitney. So Dick packed up, ate supper, and, in the absence of any news from Thornton, left for the trio's camp about six o'clock. He arrived there about nine-thirty the following morning after a twenty-six mile ride.

I had asked Siegel to let me know if Bill returned that afternoon or evening, so, having received no call by seven o'clock the next morning, I again checked with Thornton. He had found no trace of the missing man, neither had I heard from Dick, so I set out for Wallace Lake about eight o'clock. It was turning dark when I arrived. Dick heard me coming and walked down the trail to meet me.

"Gordon," he said, "I found Bill today. He's dead. Sam and I haven't told Mark yet. I figured you could handle that better than I." Then he filled me in.

That morning Dick had taken Sam with him and began a search. Sam led him to the spot on Lake Tuleinyo where Bill and he had separated. Asking Sam to stay at the lake, Dick set out to climb Mt. Russell to see if he could find some sign of Bill. Mt. Russell, on the crest of the Sierra Nevada in its highest elevations, is a twin peak. Both summits are only a few hundred feet lower than neighboring Mt. Whitney. Dick found Bill's tracks at the first summit and then followed them over to the second peak. From there he tracked Bill down the extremely dangerous north face, which drops precipitously almost a thousand feet, from 14,000 feet to 13,000 feet in elevation. About a third of the way down, Bill's tracks disappeared where his footing had apparently given away in the loose granite. (Dick mentioned that he had lost his own footing several times while tracking Bill, narrowly escaping the same fate himself.) Using his binoculars, Dick had located Bill's body about six or seven hundred feet below.

Dick had then climbed back up the north face and descended the mountain to Lake Tuleinyo, retracing his earlier route. There he had picked up Sam, and the two of them had worked their way across the talus slope which lay at the foot of the rock shield. There they found Bill's body. It had been obvious that he could not have lived long careening down that merciless slope; Dick told me that the entire top half of his skull had disappeared. They placed the body in Sam's sleeping bag and returned to camp, arriving there shortly before I did.

After receiving Dick's report, I rode on into camp, dismounted, unsaddled, and met Mark and Sam. Mark was a young man of twenty-five and Sam was twenty-nine. Bill was twenty-seven. The three of them loved the mountains and were nearing the end of a long backpack down the length of the John Muir Trail from Yosemite. All three had recently been discharged from the U. S. Navy, where they had served as officers in the Pacific. Before returning to their homes, they met in San Francisco to have a mountain adventure together.

As I fed and tied up my stock for the night, I thought about how to tell Mark about his brother. I could see that he was a fine and sensitive young man, and I wanted to be as gentle as I could about it. I knew there was no simple way to break this kind of news about a loved one. You do the best you can and hope that your own sensitivity doesn't fail you. The duty was mine, so when I had taken care of my horse and mule, I called Mark aside and told him what had happened. He took it stoically; I'm sure he had been prepared for the worst all day. I also told him that Dick and I would take a mule up next morning and get the body, but that it would be best for him to remain in camp.

Several neighboring campers joined us when we went out early next morning to pick up the body. Fortunately, we were able to get a mule within two hundred yards. When I saw Bill's half-decapitated head, I decided Mark should not see this. We left the body in the sleeping bag, draped it across the pack saddle, and cinched it down. Back in camp, I told Mark, without giving any details, that I didn't think it wise for him to see Bill. He accepted this.

Now that we had Bill's remains, what next? Everyone looked to me for an answer, as a backcountry ranger has the same responsibility in command and in duty in his district as the captain of a ship at sea. First, I wanted to get to the Mt. Whitney Ranger Station. There would be telephone communication there to help resolve matters. So Dick and I saddled the rest of our stock and rode out of the lakeside camp, headed for the Mt. Whitney Ranger Station. Mark and Sam followed afoot. It was a solemn cortege that wound its way across streams, through pines, and over the rises and falls of the mountain trail. Nonetheless, I could not help but think that for Bill, a lover of mountain splendor, this last ride of his mortal body, along a path where nature was at its finest, was fitting.

After we arrived at the ranger station about five o'clock, Dick and I took a steel cot from inside and set it down on the far side of the building. Then we placed the body on the cot. I went through Bill's pockets and gave the contents to Mark. This was the last time the sleeping bag was opened. I then called the chief ranger at park headquarters to report the accident and the action taken.

The next question was: do we pack the body down to Lone Pine or bury it here in the mountains? I opposed the Lone Pine alternative. It would take almost two days to get there. The temperatures in Owens Valley can run into three digits at that time of year, and the heat is at its worst on the exposed eastern slope of the Sierra Nevada above Lone Pine. There was no way to protect the body from decomposition. I discussed this with Mark and suggested that we bury his brother right here above Crabtree Meadow, and he agreed. He thought his brother, great lover of the mountains and appreciator of nature that he had been, would want it that way.

Next, we had to get permission. The first step was for Mark to get a connection to his father in Dover, New Hampshire, through the primitive, single, bare-wire telephone line that extended from our wilderness terminal to park headquarters. This we were able to do the first thing next morning. Mark got on the line then, and I listened to as fine an explanation of its kind as I have ever heard or read as he talked to his father. I greatly admired this young man.

Having received the father's approval, we now had to get official permission for an exception to National Park Service policy, which strictly forbids private burial in the parks. I felt we had a good case. I got Superintendent White on the line and explained the situation. He agreed at once; but he, in turn, had to get a final okay from higher authority in Washington. This came through by the time we had finished lunch.

I asked Mark if he'd like to select the burial site. He said he would leave that to me. Dick and I found a superb spot several hundred yards from the cabin. Although it was located in a grove of pines, they were widely scattered, and from there one had an unobstructed view of the creek, the meadow, the great peaks to the west, and Mt. Whitney to the east just by a turning of the head.

Dick and I set to work to dig the grave. It was very difficult. We were on a glacial moraine, and there was just about an even mix of soil and rock below the surface. Many of the rocks were so large and firmly embedded that we had to use dynamite to loosen and break them up. After several hours of hard work and blasting, we were able to dig down only about three feet. My main concern was that the grave be deep enough that a bear would not get at the body. I thought three feet would do it, so we halted there.

A short time later, Mark and Sam and Dick and I went over to the steel cot on which Bill's body was resting. Two at each end, we lifted it and, heads bared, bore it slowly down through the pines to the grave. We gently picked up the body, shrouded in its sleeping bag, and lowered it into the grave. Then the four of us hesitated.

All was quiet except for the purling of Whitney Creek as it curved and coasted down its pebbly bed immediately below the promontory of the glacial moraine on which we stood. The sun was low on the western horizon, throwing pencils of dark shadow across Crabtree Meadow below us. Its rays ignited a mellow orange fire that leaped up each of the fluted chimneys that comprise the great granite whaleback of Mt. Whitney that loomed less than a mile to the east.

Finally, I turned to Mark and said, "Would you like to say a few words, a prayer for your brother?"

Almost inaudibly, but his emotions under control, he replied, "No. But I'd like it if you would."

If I would? I was not a praying man. I had been taught to say a goodnight prayer as a child, but outgrew that before I started school. After I became a dropout from Sunday school in my teens, I probably hadn't been in a church half-a-dozen times in the twenty years since. Prayer simply wasn't a part of my life. So what to do?

I had been asked to say the final words, to utter the last prayer, for a man I hadn't known. There are times in life when you are asked to do what seems impossible. Either you rise to the occasion or you don't. A backcountry ranger has to operate principally on his own resources—there is often nobody to turn to, whatever the problem. There was no way I could let Mark down at one of the saddest moments of his life. He wanted me to pray, so I prayed. Somehow I found the words.

Dick and I filled in the grave. Next morning, Mark and Sam said goodby to us and began their hike out of the mountains down into Lone Pine. Before he completed his tour of duty at the Mt. Whitney Ranger Station ten days later, Dick, an expert wood carver, fashioned a cross out of foxtail pine, durable as concrete. It carried the name of William Penn Tuttle and the date, August 24, 1946. Few know exactly where it stands above the man who died doing what he loved best. There are many, however, who have heard the story. With the passage of almost half a century, this tragedy has passed into the lore of the High Sierra, taking on a legendary aura. It is a legend, though, based on fact, as any of the four of us who were there and still live, can testify.

For the week that followed the burial, I was engaged in the normal ebb and flow of ranger activity: patrolling to the Kern Ranger Station, cleaning up the Kern Hot Springs en route, going into Mineral King for mail and supplies, returning via Forester Lake in a snowstorm, shoeing stock, contacting tourists, and writing reports. In early September, I rode up to Chagoopa Patrol Station to camp with Superintendent White and his party, who had entered the district that morning via the High Sierra Trail over Kaweah Gap.

The colonel stayed over a day at Chagoopa and then went on down to the Kern Ranger Station, ultimately leaving the district over Coyote Pass after a three-day visit. In the meantime, I went up to the Mt. Whitney Ranger Station and helped Ranger Hester get off to Giant Forest, thus ending his summer assignment. Later in the day, I visited with a group of The Trail Riders of the Wilderness who had made camp near the station and were using the Crabtree Meadow public pasture for their stock.

The following day I patrolled to the summit of Mt.

Whitney and returned. I stuck around the station for a few more days, taking down pasture fences, with a day off to explore the Crabtree Lakes region with Dr. Jim Wortham of UCLA, before closing the Mt. Whitney Ranger Station in mid-September.

Then Mary and I set out on what was for me a sentimental return to yesteryear and for her an introduction to the area that had been my domain in 1936 and 1937. After a twenty-mile ride we camped overnight at Big Arroyo Patrol Station. Next day, we rode on over Kaweah Gap, down past Hamilton Lake, on to Bearpaw Camp, down to Redwood Meadow, up Cliff Creek, and over Timber Gap to Mineral King to complete twenty-eight magnificent miles of sightseeing. We returned to the Kern via Timber Gap, Black Rock Pass, and the Big Arroyo Patrol Station. The first day out of Mineral King, we paused briefly to extinguish a man-made fire in the Little Five Lakes area. This was a good example of the value of frequent ranger patrols, as we found an unextinguished campfire that had already destroyed seven trees and consumed about a thousand square feet of ground cover.

On September 25, with the hunting season well under way, Assistant Chief Ranger Irvin Kerr arrived at the Kern Ranger Station to help me with deer patrol. Irv was a prince of a fellow, a joy with whom to ride and camp. During the week we were together, we made a ride that no one else I know of made during the four years I was in the district.

We camped one night in Upper Rock Creek after having ridden that day up Golden Trout Creek and over Siberian Pass. After the evening meal, Irv mentioned that it might be interesting to try to locate the old Diaz Trail and follow it as far as we could. That suited me, so next morning we searched the area until we found the lower end of the trail. It was obliterated in some places, faint in others, and rough overall. It obviously had not been used or maintained for years. Nonetheless, we struggled on, and our efforts were ultimately rewarded when we emerged above timber line and rode easily up the gentle open slope of Mt. Langley to the crest of the Sierra, where we enjoyed a superlative view. We covered only seven miles that day, but they were pioneering miles that we would never forget.

It was the last day of September when Irv and I returned to the Kern Ranger Station. He took off over Coyote Pass for Mineral King the next day, while I busied myself with a few days of chopping wood in order to have a good supply on hand when I returned to the station next year. Light snow had come to the high country and fall foliage in the canyon was in its glory, all indicating that Mary's and my days in this wonderland were numbered. I made a deer patrol up to Coyote Lakes, several one-day patrols up the canyon, and one more journey to Mineral King for mail and supplies before settling down to the normal season-ending chores of dropping pasture and drift fences in the canyon. By mid-October, it had snowed twice, so I cut some more wood, burned trash, cut off the water line leading from Coyote Creek, and closed the station.

Mary and I rode the twenty-eight miles over Coyote Pass and Farewell Gap to Mineral King and on to Atwell Mill Ranger Station on one of those magnificent, crisp, bright-blue October days that grace the southern Sierra before the winter storms set in. That night we were the guests of Ace and Esther Peck. To anyone who knew this couple, just the mention of their names is enough to evoke visions of golden hours of homespun humor, warm companionship, and great food under their roof. We left the Pecks next morning and made the twenty-two mile ride down the East Fork road to Hammond and back up to the Ash Mountain Corrals to bring our season in the Kern to an end. Our stock had well earned a winter's rest; Jim had carried me almost thirteen hundred miles and Eddie had taken Mary over a thousand. Our four mules had performed no less heroically, serving as pack animals on mountain trails that, by and large, were as rugged as they come.

As can be concluded, the life and duties of a backcountry ranger in the High Sierra were many and varied. If there was anything else that a ranger might be confronted with, I am hard put to figure out what it might be. It was a tremendous experience from the beginning of the season to the end, and a major factor in making it so great was my beloved wife Mary, a true helpmate. Never having sat on a horse or lived in the mountains before, she came with me into some of the highest and most rugged country in the forty-eight states. There, with nary a complaint, she courageously conquered the isolation and inconvenience, as well as the perils that existed. She rode with me on most of my patrols and performed many chores both in camp and at the station that considerably eased my burden and made her company a delight, as always. In her new role, Mary proved to be a remarkably good sport—something I had known all along.

9

Farewell to Sequoia, Beloved Land

Upon reporting to the chief ranger after Mary and I returned from the backcountry, I learned that my new duty station was to be Ash Mountain Headquarters. When I saw the living quarters that we had been assigned, I was distressed. It was an old, one-room shanty in Poison Oak Gulch, a makeshift affair, barely habitable. The one room served as a combination living room, dining room, and bedroom. The kitchen was a small alcove at one side, and the elements of a bathroom were jammed into another space along the same side which was no more spacious than a large clothes closet.

It struck me that I was making progress in the wrong direction. From a nice, almost-new, six-room residence in Grant Grove, we had gone to a two-room log cabin in the Kern, and from there to this, not even in the same class with our Kern quarters. All in hardly more than six months after my return from military furlough. Considering my seniority and my responsibilities, it did seem that better arrangements could have been made. For the first time, I began to wonder if I had chosen the right career.

My duties during the seven months that intervened before Mary and I returned to the Kern station were pleasant enough, albeit prosaic. Most of the time I stood a shift at the checking station at the Ash Mountain entrance. This was frequently interspersed with duty in the chief ranger's office, highway patrol, and winter sports control at Wolverton and Lodgepole on weekends and holidays.

In late November, upon completing an analysis of the Kern District that I had begun late in the summer season, I submitted it to the superintendent through the chief ranger. During the course of three seasons as ranger-in-charge, I had evolved certain ideas bearing upon its administration and development, and set them down in a work I called "Suggestions for the Administration and Long-term Development of the Kern District." It was twenty-eight pages of single-space typed text, divided into seventeen sections: Introduction, Territory, Personnel, Tours of Duty, Ranger Stations, Trails, Signs, Bridges, Campgrounds, Grazing, Kern Hot Springs, Public Operator, Transportation, Communication, Sanitation, Storage, and Recapitulation of Immediate Needs. For the twenty-five hundred people who visited the Kern District in 1946, it was not the Big Trees, but the canyon and the spectacular high country on each side that comprised Sequoia National Park. With this kind of visitation, I believed more attention should be paid to the area. My effort to emphasize this was a labor of love that I had voluntarily put together to encourage a program which would lead the district to its proper position in the park. At the same time, this would be a guide of sorts not only for the present, but for the future as well.

The late fall and winter passed without unusual incident on the job, but not so on the private front. On Christmas Eve, Superintendent White gave a party for park personnel at his Ash Mountain home. Mary and I attended, but retired early after having enjoyed a very pleasant evening with our fellow workers and their families. The next day, Mary, three months pregnant, began to have pains symptomatic of a miscarriage, and by noon I had to take her to the Woodlake Hospital where she lost the child. My son, Roy, now seven, was visiting us over Christmas for the first time in his life, so things had gone badly for all three of us on this saddest of all Christmases.

Shortly after the first of the year, thoughts of my future gradually grew to a dominant position in my mind. I simply was not satisfied with what it portended in my current situation. The absence of adequate housing, the poor pay, the failure to be recognized by advancement to a rating consistent with my backcountry responsibilities, the lack of challenge during winter months, and the bleak prospect overall in a government service that was on dead center at the time, prompted me to think of taking another tack.

Because of my military service, I still had a lot of time due me on the G.I. Bill for the purpose of advancing my formal education. At first I strongly considered going for a Ph.D degree in Geography, one of my major interests. The University of Wisconsin was reputed to have one of the best, if not the very best, departments in the nation in that discipline, so I was on the verge of applying there.

About that time, Kenneth (Dane) Hansen, a fellow ranger, confided that he, too, was unhappy with things and wanted to make a move. We discussed the pros and cons at some length. He already had a bachelor's degree in geography and had taught the subject. He convinced me that there was a better way to go. His idea was to get into something that would be both challenging and profitable. I agreed. So we decided to go for the brass ring: the practice of law. The thought of becoming a criminal trial lawyer especially appealed to me.

Eventually, Dane applied for and was accepted at the University of California's Hastings College of Law in San Francisco. I went farther afield to make application at the law schools at the University of California, Berkeley; Stanford; the University of Michigan; and Harvard. I was accepted at the first three and put on standby status at Harvard.

Meanwhile, the time was rapidly approaching when I was scheduled to return to the Kern Canyon-Mt. Whitney District for the summer. I decided to put in one more season there to make certain that I would be comfortable giving up that part of my life. First, though, I was given a job to do and two young temporary employees, Vern Taylor and Jim Bates, to help me do it: making a snow survey at Hockett Meadow.

We were driven early one morning to Clough's Cave Ranger Station, where we began our trek up the South Fork Trail. We all packed lunches and some water. Vern and Jim carried skis, while I took snowshoes. None of us had been over this trail before, so we followed a topographic map as best we could. Somewhere up the line, we inadvertently branched off onto the wrong trail at a point where all appearances encouraged it. Thus, as daylight waned, we found ourselves at a small, isolated cabin instead of the Hockett Meadow Ranger Station.

I favored pushing on to Hockett Meadow where there was food, sleeping bags, and a fully equipped cabin. I now had a sense of where I was, although there was a steep ridge between us and the telephone line that ran between Quinn and Hockett. I had maintained that line the year before, so I knew that once we came to it, it would lead us on into Hockett Meadow. The snow was from two- to three-feet deep at this juncture, so I ploughed on ahead up the slope with my snowshoes to break trail while Vern and Jim struggled slowly up on skis.

By now it was dark, so I went on ahead, hoping to reach the top and locate the telephone line and trail on the other side. After a while, it appeared that it wasn't such a good idea to stumble around in the darkness, so I stopped under a large fir tree. I enlarged a space around its base to make room for a fire of dead twigs and limbs and a place to curl around it on my snowshoes. Perhaps thirty minutes later, Vern and Jim, following my tracks with a flashlight, caught up with me. They, too, carved out a space for their skis and stretched out on them. Then the three of us slept fitfully until daylight, occasionally stoking our fire to keep warm in the icy darkness.

As soon as it was light enough to see well we climbed on

up to the summit of the ridge and dropped down the other side to the telephone line. Finding it was a great relief to me, as there had been moments when I wasn't too sure I wasn't lost. Not only my own fate was at stake, but also that of the two young men who had been entrusted to my care and who in turn trusted me. In retrospect, it doesn't seem very smart to send three men many miles into a high elevation mountain wilderness, deeply covered with snow, none of whom were familiar with the way in. The stage was set for tragedy, but we avoided it.

It was a simple matter to follow the telephone line a mile or so to the cabin where we cooked breakfast and then slept until noon. We did our snow-gauging in the meadow that afternoon. Next morning, we returned by the way of the trail that led from Hockett Meadow at 8,500 feet some eleven miles on down to the Atwell Mill Ranger Station at 6,400 feet. There we were met by a ranger who drove us on into Ash Mountain, not any worse for wear, despite the peril that we had faced.

Before moving out to the Kern station, I was directed to attend a joint USFS-NPS conference in Lone Pine. The crest of the southern Sierra marks the boundary between the Inyo National Forest on the east side and Sequoia and Kings Canyon National Parks on the west. There is a great deal of trail travel that traverses both jurisdictions en route to, or returning from, various destinations in the backcountry. This is especially true of the Mt. Whitney region, where the position of the peak as the highest in the lower forty-eight states lures hundreds of visitors during the summer months. Hence, a mutuality of interest existed between these two federal agencies, made more productive by a discussion of plans and cooperation in action taken. In making that year's liaison with our counterparts on the Inyo National Forest, District Ranger Nelson Murdock represented Kings Canyon National Park and I represented Sequoia National Park.

Finally, on May 6, 1947, Mary and I and Jim, Caesar, Kitten, Babe, Bill, Buck, Sally, Kate, and Skeeter were transported by truck to Quaking Aspen Meadow. Next morning, accompanied by a trail crew of four, we began our two-day migration to the Kern Ranger Station. This entourage presented a far different scene than Mary's and my lonely entrance into the Kern Canyon the year before.

Also, what we found at the station when we arrived was as different from last year as white is from black. The cabin, inside and out, and the surrounding grounds were as spotless and orderly as we had left them in the fall. Furthermore, I now had a trail crew to assist me right from the beginning. The foreman, Alexander Douglas, newly hired, took hold at once and handled his job in an excellent manner. Since I had work for them to do around the station, they established their camp nearby after unpacking and putting up the pasture fence at Lewis Camp.

Reminiscent of the Dawson incident in 1941, Vernon Weekley, one of the trail crew came down with an unknown malady on the fourth day after arrival in the canyon. It did not appear life-threatening, but it seemed serious enough that I wanted to get him out to medical attention right away. He, too, wanted to leave. Hence, the next day I took him all the way back to Quaking Aspen where I arranged for a park vehicle to pick him up.

Knowing that there were still supplies awaiting at Quaking Aspen for myself and the trail crew, I had taken three mules with me. Next morning I packed them and rode back the twenty-six miles to the station that same day. Meanwhile, the trail crew had been busy: digging a garbage pit, cutting and stacking a two-year supply of firewood, cleaning up campgrounds, putting up fences, and working nearby trails.

In late May, I moved them up to Upper Funston Meadow, where they began work on the High Sierra Trail. I took Douglas with me up to Skyparlor Meadow on the Chagoopa Plateau and as far up Rattlesnake Canyon toward Franklin Pass as we could get to instruct him on fencing pastures and maintaining high country trails. Confident that Douglas understood what was required, I left him to do his job and returned to the Kern Ranger Station at the end of the month. I made out my monthly report for May and took it in with me when Mary and I rode back to Quaking Aspen to pick up mail and more supplies for ourselves and the trail crew.

I had learned that the two sets of coil springs and innerspring mattresses that I had listed as an immediate need in my long report of the previous November would also be awaiting us at Quaking Aspen, so I had come in with a string of seven mules. Two of these I turned over to the two young men who had appeared as replacements for the trail crew members who had already quit. We all laid over the next day to organize packs for the trip back to the Kern Ranger Station.

It was simple enough to get the packs of supplies loaded and cinched down on several of the mules, but the springs and mattresses presented a real challenge. Nonetheless, with the help of my wife, the two tenderfeet, and a lot of ingenuity, I got the job done. It was the apex of my mule-packing days, crowned by making the entire twenty-six mile journey over rough mountain trails without having to pause to make changes in the packs. Thus it was that Mary and I had good beds for the rest of our sojourn in the Kern, as did those who followed us in later years—long before helicopters were in use.

All through June and well into July, my duties were routine. Although mainly a repetition of 1946, my patrols were not as frequent because I made only occasional inspection and instructional contact with the trail crew, instead of having to work the trails myself. Moreover, Dick Hester returned to resume his position of temporary ranger at his old stand at the foot of Mt. Whitney. In company with his wife, he reported to me at the Kern Ranger Station and went on almost at once to open his station in late June, a full month earlier than he had come on duty in 1946. That, plus the experience he had gained and confidence I had in him earned by his performance the previous summer, relieved me of the necessity to duplicate the long and arduous patrols and sundry duties in that area that were my lot in 1946.

On July 6, I rode into Mineral King and next day drove to Los Angeles to bring my son back with me to the Kern for the remainder of his summer vacation. Although we had only two saddle horses for the three of us, I taught him to ride, and we covered a lot of territory in the following two months. This was Roy's initiation into the backcountry and his first visit of any length with his father. It was a wonderful time for both of us and for Mary, who developed a mother's affection for her stepson.

Mary had already spent five months in the backcountry with me in 1946, so she was somewhat at home in the mountains. But up to now, she had had no "close encounters of the third kind" as represented by animals and reptiles. This changed one day when she had ascended the throne in our outhouse in response to a call of nature. Once settled, she sensed an alien presence and turned her attention to a partially darkened section of the privy. There, virtually within arm's reach, was a large rattlesnake coiled cozily in the corner. It had not rattled. It did not need to, because Mary was up and out of there as if shot from a cannon, momentarily in immodest dishabille.

On another occasion, I left Mary and Roy at the station while I made an overnight trip into Mineral King for mail and supplies. Sometime during the night, Mary was awakened by a commotion at our burlap-covered evaporative food cooler that hung on high from one of the protruding logs at one side of the cabin. Grabbing a flashlight that was at hand and stopping by the closet to take my Smith and Wesson .38 Special from the shelf, she ventured courageously outside to confront whatever might be the marauder. It was a full-grown American black bear, intent on a midnight snack. Mary pointed the flashlight at him with one hand and the gun with the other, ready to do whatever she had to do to protect our perishables. The bear presumably got the message when he saw the gun, because he departed in great haste. Mary didn't know, though, that the gun was unloaded until I told her after hearing about her escapade. But then, the bear didn't know this either.

Mary has many fine attributes. Among them is her dedication and competence as a cook. She is good, and one reason

THE KERN RANGER WITH HIS WIFE AND SON

PLAYTIME IN THE KERN
(RANGER WALLACE WITH FAMILY AND FRIENDS)

for this is that she tries not to run out of essential foodstuffs. One day we ran out of butter. The next day was Sunday, and I had work to do at the station, so I was there when Mary announced she would ride the eight miles up Golden Trout Creek to the little store at Tunnel Meadow to see if she could procure some. Alas, the supply there was exhausted. But Bob White nearby heard about her problem and thought he had an answer.

Bob was the commercial pilot who regularly flew hunters and fishermen and other frequenters of the backcountry into Tunnel Meadow from Lone Pine. He happened to be on the verge of flying back to Lone Pine to pick up a load of gear for some fishermen he had just brought in, so he offered Mary a ride to town. She was frustrated once more when she found all the food stores closed on Sunday in this surprisingly civilized little town in the Owens Valley. Seemingly defeated in her quest, she returned empty-handed to Tunnel Meadow with Bob White. However, on the way back to the Kern, she stopped a few moments to chat with a fisherman in Little Whitney Meadow. This was his last day in the mountains, so upon hearing of her plight, he gave Mary all the butter that remained in his pack—at least a pound. When Mary came riding into the station, I was amazed to hear of her odyssey, flying far afield in quest of butter, and the irony of her final success only four short miles from home.

Things were going smoothly in the district. Travel in the canyon was not as heavy as last year, but it had increased in the Whitney region. Fishing in the Kern River was the finest in many years. The Mt. Whitney trail was in the best shape possible, short of actual reconstruction, and it had drawn considerable favorable comment. Fire-suppression activity was minimal; whereas last year some of my time and energy was devoted to fighting a number of fires, this year only one had broken out.

This particular fire originated from an unextinguished campfire at the campsite on the Kern River just a few hundred yards north of the drift fence near the Rock Creek confluence. It was discovered at 12:45 P.M. on July 25 by three men who were hiking along the Kern Canyon trail, and they attacked it immediately with water. By four o'clock they had it under control. Considerable damage might have resulted in the absence of the laborious efforts of this trio of hikers. Toward evening a party of eight stopped to camp there and relieved the original firefighters. They, in turn, quenched all further outbreaks during the night and next morning. When I arrived early next day, all that needed to be done was a little mopping up. About twenty-five hundred square feet had burned, but damage was negligible. The bad news here was the careless disregard of campfire safety by one party; the good news was the prompt initiative of the discoverers in containing the fire. Fortunately, there were many more visitors of the latter type traversing such garden spots as the Kern Canyon than there were of the former.

With the month of July almost gone, it was time to bite the bullet. Resignation from my National Park Service position had been on my mind for months, as I mulled over the pros and cons. I could not reasonably postpone giving Superintendent White notice of my intentions. He had sent me a memorandum in early June informing me that he and Assistant Superintendent Carlson were both working on the official reallocation of my position to district ranger. I appreciated this effort, but was skeptical that it would produce results any time soon. Anyhow, if I were to make a break, the time was now. I knew by this point, two-and-a-half months into my fourth season as the *de facto* district ranger, that, under the circumstances that existed, I had met all the challenges that the district had to offer and had put it into the best shape possible. Given this, even the tremendous appeal of living and working in this mountain wonderland faded when viewed in the light of an unknown number of summers that apparently stretched ahead of me, marking time as it were, and the even-less-inviting killing of time at routine duties during the winter off-seasons.

I had received official notifications from the Stanford Law

School and the University of California School of Jurisprudence at Berkeley that my applications for admission had been accepted. So the road was clear. I wanted to discuss these developments with Superintendent White and had looked forward to doing so on the trip he planned into the district in July. However, the busiest year ever in the parks had kept him at his desk at headquarters. I wanted to give him sixty days notice of my intentions, so, in lieu of being able to discuss this with him personally, I wrote him a letter on July 28, outlining my thinking. He answered on August 4, expressing complete sympathy for my purpose, although "very sorry to lose you," and wishing me every success.

Bulking large on the downside of leaving Sequoia National Park was the termination of my official relationship with Colonel John R. White. He was my mentor and my friend, and I admired him greatly. He was as near a role model as I had at that stage in my life. Among his many attributes were courage, dedication, intelligence, honesty, ability, and true interest in and consideration for others. As things turned out, however, he retired just one month after my resignation took effect. Later, we became neighbors in the San Francisco Bay area, and our relationship continued warm and close throughout the remaining years of his remarkable life.

There was one bit of business that I wanted very much to finish before I left the district. In my long report of November 20, 1946, I had made much of the poor situation at Kern Hot Springs and recommended certain improvements. Unlike the previous year, when I had no trail crew or other personnel to divert to improving the situation, this year I had some help. So I pulled the crew off trail maintenance for a short spell in mid-August and put them to work at the Hot Springs. Following my instructions, and with Ranger Hester on the spot to give them guidance and assistance, they first removed the old shakes from the bathhouse, reinforced the frame, and placed new cedar shakes on the roof and walls. They then built a corduroy log walk over the boggy area and erected a rustic rail fence around the entire site. This was a great improvement that took care of much that I had in mind. Now I could rest easy that this spot, the most popular in the canyon, if not the entire district, could speak decently for the park as a whole.

On August 24, Fred Paget entered the Rock Creek area to make final plans for the erection of a snow-survey cabin for the state. I dispatched Ranger Hester to meet him with instructions that, in line with NPS policy, there would be no more than a minimal cutting of trees, nor was the cabin itself to be visible from any part of the trail. I had a telephone conversation with Mr. Paget before he went into Rock Creek and again after he returned to Lone Pine. He showed every indication of full cooperation. In the meantime Hester had assisted him in marking the trees to be cut and choosing the cabin site. The actual construction was planned for the following year.

On September 1, I patrolled to Big Whitney Meadow and the next day met The Trail Riders of the Wilderness in Rock Creek. Twenty-five strong, they had been brought in over Army Pass by Ike Livermore, operator and owner of the Mt. Whitney Pack Trains, with thirty head of pack stock in tow. This visit was of particular interest to me, because Shirley Allen was in charge of this group. He was a Professor of Forestry at the University of Michigan, where I had elected to take his course in Forest Administration when I was completing my undergraduate studies there just eighteen months before.

Shirley Allen was a fine professor, an authority in his field, and a regular guy, so it was a real pleasure to see him again and move our relationship from his classroom to my wilderness domain. The next morning, I rode with him and his Trail Riders over Guyot Pass to Mt. Whitney Ranger Station, where they camped for several days. Mary and Roy and I were making shift with only two saddle horses, so Ike Livermore kindly made one of his available to us for the ride to the summit of Mt. Whitney with Allen and his people.* It was also a red-letter day for my son, who made the ascent of Mt. Whitney less than a week after his eighth birthday.

Ranger Hester and his wife departed that same morning for Giant Forest to close out his short-lived NPS career, inasmuch as he was due to resume his studies in geology at UCLA. I remained with the Trail Riders for several nights, joining with Forester Carlock Johnson in making informal campfire talks before returning to the Kern Ranger Station. Several days later the Trail Riders departed the park over Siberian Pass.

Matters were now rapidly coming to a head. Mary and Roy and I, with our two horses, took two days to return the twenty-eight miles to Mt. Whitney Ranger Station to the Kern Ranger Station, and the following day, September 7, went on twenty-two miles over Coyote Pass and Farewell Gap to Mineral King. I then took two days off to drive Roy back to Los Angeles, so he could start school.

In the meantime, three members of the trail crew requested that they be relieved of their duties as of September 5, and Foreman Douglas, now alone, moved on down to the Kern Ranger Station on September ninth. This was the same day that Ray Buckman moved the Neelands out of their camp and store at Lewis Camp to close out the operation for the season. When I returned from Los Angeles, I was placed on duty at Ash Mountain Headquarters for two days while my replacement, Ranger Ruben O. Lundberg, readied himself to go back to the Kern with us. Park Naturalist Howard Stagner was also scheduled to go in with us on a familiarization patrol

---

*Norman B. Livermore Jr., known to all simply as "Ike," did me an even greater favor twenty years later when he selected me to be his assistant leader on a Sierra Club saddle trip he was scheduled to lead over the Kern Plateau. This opened the door, in 1967, for my leadership of more than a score of wilderness treks and commercial deluxe tours that took me all over the world in the following seven years. Our mutual interests, born long along in the High Sierra, have bound us together in a friendship that is stronger than ever today.

through the district. Thus it was that on September 12, Lundberg, Stagner, Mary, and I rode out of Mineral King over Farewell Gap to the Kern Ranger Station.

The assignment of Ranger Lundberg to replace me was a prime example of the strange twists that life interweaves between two people in playing out their destinies for them. I was twenty and Lundy was twenty-five when, in 1930, we met while working in a lumber mill near Burns on the fringe of the high sagebrush desert of eastern Oregon. Lundy was a grader and I was a lumber-handler; we became well-acquainted when we occasionally worked as a team in the shipping department to fill orders for "select" grade lumber.

Both of us moved on when the Depression made our jobs untenable, and we lost track of one another. One evening, a full ten years later, I was on duty at the Ash Mountain Checking Station when Lundy drove up. What a pleasant surprise! He had been to a reserve officers' meeting in nearby Visalia and was returning over the Generals Highway to his station at Grant Grove in Kings Canyon National Park. This park had just been established, and its administration was separate from that of Sequoia National Park. Thus I had no idea that he, too, was now a ranger. Our paths crossed again in Arkansas, during World War II, and when I returned from military furlough, I had even taken over his old station in Grant Grove for several months. He returned to the parks, now consolidated, after I had gone into the Kern in 1946, and was assigned duties at Ash Mountain. So here we were, old friends, interlocked again by the movement of events.*

Lundberg and Stagner remained at the station for several days while I briefed the former on his duties. Then the two of them, led by Trail Foreman Douglas, rode off on an extensive patrol to become acquainted with the district. Lundberg closed the Mt. Whitney Ranger Station on September eigh-

---

*Hence, it did not seem strange to us when Lundy resigned from the NPS seven months later and followed me to the Bay area, became my neighbor, and an even closer friend as he operated his own lumber business for many years in my new hometown of San Rafael.

teen, before they returned to the Kern Ranger Station on September twenty-fourth.

Meanwhile, I stayed at the station. There were written reports to be made and other matters to be attended to, connected with my departure from the district. Mary and I left the Kern Ranger Station for Mineral King on September twenty-fifth. It was our last horseback ride for many years, one that made my total for the season 952 miles and Mary's 565; even Roy logged 288 miles.

After long deliberation, I had chosen Stanford from among those that had accepted me as best fitted to meet my objectives. There was no time to lose, as classes were to begin at the end of September. That gave us only a day or two to find a place to live in the Palo Alto area. Moving was no problem, as everything we owned fit into our automobile. My official resignation took effect September thirtieth. (Ranger Hansen had resigned several weeks earlier to begin classes at Hastings College of Law.)

I had mixed emotions about leaving Sequoia National Park. I had spent the finest years of my life there, highlighted by six marvelous seasons as a backcountry ranger in an extraordinarily beautiful, spectacular, and spiritually stimulating environment. I was privileged to have had this experience, and I knew it. The physical element was a paradise I was loath to leave, but at this point certain things that made me tick were missing. Novelty and challenge no longer existed, and opportunity appeared to be nowhere in sight. So, the time had come to move on. Thus it was that I bade farewell to Sequoia, beloved land.

Epilogue

The old ranger stood on top of Moro Rock. The frosts of more than eighty winters had turned his hair white, but this was mostly hidden by the same ranger Stetson that he had worn there half-a-century before. Tall and trim, his figure had changed very little in that time, and his mind remained alert and his movements vigorous. Dressed in the garb of a Volunteer in Parks, the similarity to that of a park ranger drew a number of questions from the tourists who had climbed up for the view. He was in his element. It was just like the good old times for three or four hours that Sunday in late July 1990, as he fielded questions with a knowledge based on his extensive experience with everything in sight.

Immediately to the north, the Big Trees and other magnificent conifers bulked large and dense, sweeping eastward up the breast of the Sierra to Panther Gap, ultimately fading away on the open slopes of Alta Peak. Below Moro Rock the Middle Fork of the Kaweah River dropped down its canyon from the east, having drained for its cascading waters the springs and melting snows of the Great Western Divide at its head. As high as this mighty range of 12,000-feet peaks loomed on the eastern horizon, they could not obscure on their far side the tips of the Black and Red Kaweah in the Kern watershed, close to 14,000 feet in height.

Between the crest of the Divide and the canyon below Moro Rock was a honeycomb of trails that the old ranger knew as well as the back of his hand, for he had ridden two thousand miles to and fro in this area. This had kept him in constant communication with such shrines as Bearpaw Meadow Camp, the Valhalla, Angel's Wing, Hamilton Lake, Kaweah Gap, Cliff Creek, Black Rock Pass, and Timber Gap. In the midst of all this rested his old home at Redwood Meadow.

Continuing his inspection clockwise, the old ranger followed Paradise Ridge to the south, down past Castle Rocks and Milk Ranch Peak, which towered above Ash Mountain Headquarters. Below this little community, the Middle Fork was lost in the summer haze of the San Joaquin Valley as it wound its way westward. Then his eyes picked up the Generals Highway below the Ash Peaks and followed it up the river to Hospital Rock. From Moro Rock, the old ranger let his eyes follow every curve and turn of this magnificent road as it switchbacked up the mountain side to Amphitheater Point and Deer Ridge, where it disappeared from sight, buried in the fastness of the Giant Forest. If one may be allowed a bit of poetic license, one could say that he knew this road well enough to drive it blind-folded, for he had driven it a hundred times and more.

Yes, the 360-degree view from the summit of Moro Rock was one that meant more to the old ranger than any he had known in all his travels. He had either visited or lived in all fifty states and more than three-score countries on all continents except Antarctica. This had enabled him to climb, ride, canoe, raft, and ski in the Canadian, Idaho, and Wyoming Rockies; the Oregon Cascades; the Grand Canyon of the Colorado; the European and Japanese Alps; the volcanoes of Central Mexico; the Peruvian Andes; the Tasmanian Wilderness; the highland jungles of Papua New Guinea; the far outposts of Northern Pakistan where the Himalaya, the Karakoram, and the Hindu Kush meet in Hunzaland; the Kashmir Himalaya in India; and across five lateral ranges of the Himalaya in Nepal to the top of Kala Patar, at 18,500 feet just above the base camp of Mt. Everest expeditions. This had all been wonderfully fulfilling, but always the old ranger returned to Sequoia, because no scenes in all the world were more dear to his heart than those he knew here so well.

That is why, during more than forty years, the old ranger had returned many times, including eight trips into the backcountry, to these scenes that were once a part of his daily life. A powerful magnet drew him, sometimes alone, sometimes to share this special place with family or friends. The attraction was irresistible.

Yes, the old ranger left his beloved Sequoia many years ago, but it never left him.